Future-Ready Teaching With AI

"It's no longer a question. AI will transform education. So, then, how might we best navigate this brave new world in education? This timely book provides a timely answer. We must learn to embrace the powerful potential of AI in the classroom, and Aaron Blackwelder and Jason Cowley's work here shows us the way. A must-own for today's educator in tomorrow's world (which is already here)."

—Monte Syrie, 28-year veteran of
the high school English classroom and
author of *better: A Teacher's Journey*

Future-Ready Teaching With AI

Unlocking Student Potential in the Age of Artificial Intelligence

Aaron Blackwelder

Jason Cowley

FOR INFORMATION:

Corwin

A SAGE Company

2455 Teller Road

Thousand Oaks, California 91320

(800) 233-9936

www.corwin.com

SAGE Publications Ltd.

1 Oliver's Yard

55 City Road

London EC1Y 1SP

United Kingdom

SAGE Publications India Pvt. Ltd.

Unit No 323-333, Third Floor, F-Block

International Trade Tower Nehru Place

New Delhi 110 019

India

SAGE Publications Asia-Pacific Pte. Ltd.

18 Cross Street #10-10/11/12

China Square Central

Singapore 048423

Vice President and
  Editorial Director: Monica Eckman

Senior Acquisitions Editor: Liz Gildea

Content Development
  Editor: Melissa Rostek

Product Associate: Zachary Vann

Project Editor: Amy Schroller

Copy Editor: Diana Breti

Typesetter: C&M Digitals (P) Ltd.

Cover Designer: Candice Harman

Marketing Manager: Margaret O'Connor

Printed in the United States of America

Library of Congress Cataloging-in-Publication Data

Names: Blackwelder, Aaron, author. | Cowley, Jason, author.

Title: Future-ready teaching with AI : unlocking student potential in the age of artificial intelligence / Aaron Blackwelder, Jason Cowley.

Other titles: Future-ready teaching with artificial intelligence

Description: Thousand Oaks, California : Corwin, [2025] | Series: Corwin teaching essentials; vol 1 | Includes bibliographical references and index.

Identifiers: LCCN 2024039329 | ISBN 9781071949641 (paperback ; acid-free paper) | ISBN 9781071973769 (epub) | ISBN 9781071973776 (epub) | ISBN 9781071973783 (pdf)

Subjects: LCSH: Artificial intelligence—Educational applications. | Effective teaching.

Classification: LCC LB1028.43 .B594 2025 | DDC 371.30285/63—dc23/eng/20241106
LC record available at https://lccn.loc.gov/2024039329

This book is printed on acid-free paper.

25 26 27 28 29 10 9 8 7 6 5 4 3 2 1

CONTENTS

Please visit the authors' companion website for
Future-Ready Teaching With AI.
www.beyondthecurriculum.net/book-1

ACKNOWLEDGMENTS

Writing is a collaborative effort and many people helped us along the way. The authors would like to thank the following people: Tori Bachman, Liz Gildea, the entire team at Corwin, Sara Johnson, Tyler Mckell, Matt Greco, Matthew Johnson, Shari Conditt, Steve Rippl, Heidi Blackwelder, and Heather Cowley.

Finally, thank you to all of the students and educators who challenged us to explore the possibilities of education.

PUBLISHER'S ACKNOWLEDGMENTS

Corwin gratefully acknowledges the contributions of the following reviewers:

Michael Drezek
District Technology Integrator, Lake Shore CSD
Angola, NY

Carol S. Holzberg
Pre-K-12 Educational Technology Consultant, Warwick Public Schools
Warwick, MA

Serena Pariser
Educator/Author
Saint Louis Park, MN

Brett Vogelsinger
English Teacher, Central Bucks School District
Doylestown, PA

ABOUT THE AUTHORS

Aaron Blackwelder has taught middle and high school English, served as a digital learning coach, and coached both boys' and girls' high school golf. He co-founded Teachers Going Gradeless, hosts the podcast *Beyond the Curriculum,* and contributes to *Spectrum Life Magazine.*

Aaron was a Washington State English Teachers Fellow, a 2019 Washington State Teacher of the Year nominee, and a five-time golf coach of the year.

As a digital learning coach, Aaron encourages teachers to incorporate technology to promote twenty-first-century learning. He has also led professional development on the transformative power of AI in the classroom. In his teaching, he empowers students to leverage digital tools through student-centered, project-based learning.

Aaron is a husband and father of two boys on the autism spectrum who inspire him to meet the needs of all students.

**Jason Cowley** is a National Board–Certified ELA teacher and a former instructional coach with more than eighteen years of experience in the classroom. He also worked as a National Board facilitator for eight years. In addition to his work on AI in the classroom, Jason has extensively studied how assessment practices impact student learning.

When ChatGPT became popular, Jason started using AI in his classroom with students. He conducted action research measuring how to improve student writing using ChatGPT. Jason has shared his findings with large groups and with smaller PLCs.

Jason has collaborated with educators on how to integrate generative AI into classrooms and how teachers can use generative AI to support their own work. Jason works as a high school ELA teacher.

He lives with his wife and children in Vancouver, Washington.

INTRODUCTION

In November 2022, ChatGPT-3 took the Internet by storm. Many declared that it would change the world (O'Malley, 2023). However, fears began circulating among teachers that generative artificial intelligence (GenAI) such as ChatGPT would enable students to cheat, thus opening a Pandora's box that would destroy the teaching of writing across all content areas. Though GenAI can certainly generate code, develop a slide presentation on the metamorphosis of a butterfly, and write a decent five-paragraph essay outlining the character development of Atticus Finch in *To Kill a Mockingbird*, it will not diminish the need for students to learn essential skills. Like any other technological innovation, it will, however, change how we teach and will ask us to develop new essential skills.

Monolithic technology is not new to teaching. Consider spellcheck, the graphing calculator, Internet search engines, and typing vs. handwriting. When these technologies were first introduced teachers expressed their concerns. They worried students would not need to learn essential skills and traditional learning would become obsolete. But as teachers learned how to leverage these tools they became essential components in our classrooms. Teachers no longer worry that Google will destroy research skills. Instead, we teach students how to effectively keyword search to find the relevant information they need. The Internet has not dumbed down education; rather, it allows students and teachers to be better informed. And since the advent of the smartphone, we can acquire up-to-date information about any topic whenever we want and wherever we are.

A common byproduct of new technologies in education is efficiency, which helps afford us time to do more meaningful things. Take spellcheck, for example. Spellcheck did not displace the need to learn how to spell. It helps us write more clearly and communicate our ideas more effectively. Teachers of writing whose students use spell check no longer need to highlight and comment on spelling errors. Instead, time can be spent commenting on the ideas of the writing to help promote deeper thinking. Not having to mark grammatical errors allows teachers to ask probing questions on student essays that enables students to expand upon their writing. Tools such as spellcheck have also helped make writing more accessible for language learners and students with IEPs by decreasing the amount of effort students need to spend on correcting spelling and grammar.

This book will help teachers leverage GenAI in their practice to streamline the rudimentary tasks we do regularly, such as lesson planning, assessment, and differentiating materials, in order to free up time to do more meaningful work such as building relationships, providing thought-provoking feedback, and personalizing learning to support the growth of all students in our classrooms. This is not a "how to use AI" book. Although we provide some instruction on AI tools, the intent of this book is to move teachers beyond basic use of AI and help them raise rigor, increase engagement, and promote more meaningful learning opportunities in their classrooms.

The book addresses the following topics:

- Understanding generative AI

- Empowering teachers with generative AI

- Supporting student learning with generative AI

- Ethical uses of generative AI

- Shifting pedagogy with generative AI

Each chapter starts with a narrative from either Aaron or Jason that shares their personal experience with GenAI as educators. These are meant to help humanize the role of AI in education. Each chapter concludes with a chapter review that highlights the main takeaways from the chapter, a You Try It activity to help readers apply some of the strategies learned in the chapter, and reflective questions that can be used to help readers grapple with some of the challenging topics in the book or to facilitate book studies within professional learning communities. Finally, a QR code and URL will be included to link teachers to resources mentioned in the book.

CHAPTER 1

UNDERSTANDING GENERATIVE AI

A Message From Aaron

As a digital learning coach whose job it is to support teachers and students as they navigate the ever-changing technological landscape, I often have conversations with educators about artificial intelligence (AI). Many are skeptical and worry about how it will change education. Will it make teachers obsolete? What about cheating? How do we ensure students will meet state learning outcomes? Others are curious and want to learn what it is and how it can be used. Either way, I tell people, AI is a tool like a hammer or blender. It lacks any moral compass and can only do what it is programmed to do. And like any other tool, it is designed to make life easier by streamlining day-to-day tasks. Like a hammer, it can be used to build or destroy. It depends upon who is using it and their intentions.

It is good to have a healthy skepticism around AI—asking questions about authenticity and how it might be used to create content designed to deceive. And like most technology, it will replace certain jobs. But the fear that AI will take over the world, at this point in time, is irrational. Back in the 1970s assembly lines became more and more automated. This led to many assembly line workers losing their jobs, and cities such as Detroit were hit hard. People feared a robot takeover. Popular films such as Blade Runner presented a bleak future where androids were banned from Earth and hunted down and killed because they were seen as a threat to humanity.

Needless to say, robots did not take over humanity nor did they replace us in the workforce. At the time of writing this book, there is

(Continued)

(Continued)

a labor shortage. In 2022, for example, according to the United States Chamber of Commerce, we had 1.5 million fewer Americans participating in the labor force than in previous years. Robots and AI are not making humans obsolete. Rather, the labor shortage suggests that there is still a need for human labor. Like the automation revolution of the 1970s, the advent of new technology has transformed the workplace and its demands. Jobs requiring manual labor were replaced by jobs that require human interaction. The number of careers in computer programming, data security, and the energy sector increased, for example. The arrival of AI will further transform the nature of work, which means education—how and what we teach to prepare our students for the real world outside our classrooms—needs to be reimagined.

I remember having a conversation with Jason sometime back in 2018. He asked me for my thoughts on the potential of a computer or machine being able to write essays for students. My response was not what one would expect of an English teacher. I said, "Jason, I hate mowing my lawn and I pay someone to come to my house and mow my lawn every week. No one in my neighborhood complains about this. They don't call me a fraud because I have someone help me make my home look nice. Though I don't claim to mow the lawn, I do take credit for my home's appearance and I am quite proud of my home. I know some of my neighbors mow their own lawns and take joy in doing so. I can't stand mowing my lawn so I outsource it.

Now that we have arrived at a point when writing can be done by a computer, we will have to embrace the fact that some students will want to learn to write and find joy in the writing process while others will find it grueling and will want to avoid it at all costs. Students will eventually have the option to do the writing themselves or outsource it. However, both types of students will need to be taught how to be responsible for the content the computer generates and understand the ethics and rules around using that type of content. We will have to teach students to be more critical thinkers when this technology arrives."

Fast forward a few years and the technology is here. Students have the option to either complete certain tasks themselves or have AI do it for them. Educators face the challenge of a paradigm shift that no longer relies on outcomes, but rather the process and critical thinking of the outcomes.

This book discusses the impact of AI on teaching and learning and provides a vision for the future of education. Not only will it suggest tools to support you, but it will also offer a lens to help frame the potential of teaching and learning in the age of AI.

Aaron

AI IS TRANSFORMING EDUCATION

AI will forever change the scope of education, paving the way for more inclusive and equitable learning environments. This book equips educators to become leaders in this transformation, demonstrating how to harness the power of AI to empower every student, regardless of background or learning style.

Imagine a classroom where

- **AI tutors** personalize instruction for students who need accommodations, offering text-to-speech conversion or visual aids to enhance comprehension.

- **AI-powered practice tools** can assist students from low-income backgrounds, offering tutoring with targeted practice activities and links to additional resources to bridge any achievement gaps.

- **AI-powered learning platforms** curate personalized learning journeys for students in rural areas, offering adaptive learning materials, interactive simulations, and connections with online mentors, breaking down geographical barriers to learning and creating a world of possibilities within the classroom walls.

This book delves into the practical applications of AI in the classroom, exploring how it can empower teachers to meet diverse student learning needs and prepare students to engage in a world that expects them to be AI literate.

However, we must acknowledge the importance of responsible AI implementation. This book also addresses critical issues of data privacy, the limitations of AI, and how to ensure the technology remains a complementary tool rather than a replacement for human educators.

By embracing AI literacy, educators can create a future in which every student has access to a high-quality, personalized education. This book equips teachers with the knowledge and tools to become leaders in this exciting new age.

WHAT IS GENERATIVE AI?

When we think of AI in science fiction, we often think of robots fighting humanity. In these stories robots become sentient and an uprising follows. This is a common misconception about AI. Researchers term this kind of AI *artificial general intelligence* (Rogers, 2023). It is important to understand that when talking about AI in education and generative AI (a.k.a. GenAI) specifically, we are *not* talking about artificial general intelligence. Generative AI is something entirely different.

HOW GENERATIVE AI WORKS

Before we go any further, we will share a simple overview of how generative AI works. This will help ensure that we have common definitions for the terms listed below, as they will come up frequently throughout the rest of the book.

Generative AI: Generative AI is called *generative* because ultimately it is used to generate something (text, pictures, other media) in response to a prompt. *Generative* describes what it does but not the process by which it completes a task. Generative AI works by recognizing patterns and then predicting what the likeliest response to a prompt would be. Generative AI that you are familiar with probably includes text-producing AI like Open AI's ChatGPT or Google's Gemini.

Large Language Models: Generative AI is based on Large Language Models (LLMs), so named because they are trained by "reading" a lot of text or other data. An article from the website Science Focus claims ChatGPT-3 was trained by using 570 GB, or 300 billion words, of text (Hughes, 2023). According to back-of-the-napkin math, that is the equivalent of reading 3 million novels! Websites like Wikipedia, books, social media sites like Reddit, and other sources were used to train these LLMs. While the scope of ChatGPT-3 is massive, ChatGPT-4 is estimated to be more than 10 times larger! It is estimated that ChatGPT-4 contains more than 1.8 trillion parameters and was trained on 13 trillion tokens (Walker, 2023).

Transformers: LLMs read the text and run it in through something called a transformer. (The GPT in ChatGPT stands for "generative pretrained transformer.") The transformer spots words and patterns and then makes predictions about what words or phrases might come next. This is commonly seen in predictive text on a cell phone, but it works at an even stronger level with the transformer. For example, given the phrase "On Sunday, I mowed my ______", the transformer would likely predict that, based on the text it has read, *lawn* or *yard* would have a high probability of being the next word in that sentence. It isn't likely to produce a sentence about mowing your *flamingo* because the text the LLMs were trained on makes no mention of mowing flamingos (unless one regularly mows a lot of flamingos and writes about it). It is important to understand that LLMs don't "know" that lawns are mowed and flamingos are not. It predicts that based on the text it has read. Generative AI that produces images, video, and audio largely functions the same.

Usually, LLMs are further refined by human operators who fix mistakes and create rules for generative AI to follow. This is why the largest generative AIs will refuse to answer certain questions or prompts.

Chatbots: A chatbot is the interface users interact with while using generative AI. Users can have a conversation with a chatbot and receive information based on their inputs that the transformers read and respond to accordingly. Examples include ChatGPT, Google Gemini, and Microsoft Copilot.

Generative AI predicts a response based on its programming, but it doesn't have an awareness of the meaning behind what is said. This is important because it means that even though generative AI can answer questions and hold a conversation, it doesn't understand what it is saying. This has huge implications. Generative AI cannot distinguish between accurate and inaccurate information. Also, it can generate a combination of false and true information (known as *hallucination*); for example, it may cite real authors and publications but make up statistics.

For example, while researching writing instruction, one of the most widely used GenAI platforms was asked the following question: "Are there data or statistics you can find indicating how popular formulaic writing instruction is in K–12 education in the United States?" The response from GenAI contained the following information: "A 2016 survey of English teachers found that 72% of them reported using formulaic writing instruction in their classrooms" (Google, 2023). This sounds like great information from a highly respected source. Unfortunately, when pressed, GenAI was unable to provide a link or any further information on the study. Searching the NCTE website was equally fruitless. In this case, it appears highly likely that GenAI manufactured plausible-sounding data. A more recent repetition of the original question yielded different statistics and studies that the GenAI was once again unable to cite, find, or link to. Thus generative AI, especially the text-based LLMs, have the potential to be the world's greatest con artists: They sound intelligent and convincing, but they don't understand anything they are saying.

EXAMPLES OF GENERATIVE AI

The prevalence of GenAI is on the rise, finding its way into various tools like search engines, social media platforms, and other industry tools. Its integration aims to simplify and enhance user experiences, leading to significant transformations in how people work. With GenAI, users can now effortlessly generate new content, ideas, and designs, ranging from realistic images to videos and innovative solutions, making it an indispensable aspect of the modern workplace.

By streamlining routine tasks such as writing emails, crafting presentations, and producing tutorial videos, GenAI significantly boosts workplace productivity. Employing automation and intelligent algorithms, it can efficiently create reports, analyze data, and perform complex calculations, ultimately saving time and minimizing human effort.

Creative blocks are common hurdles for artists, causing ideas to feel elusive and inspiration to wane. GenAI platforms offer a valuable remedy by providing an abundance of inspiration. Designers can explore the vast array of generated content on these platforms, gaining fresh perspectives and sparking ideas that reignite their creative processes.

One of the most valuable contributions of GenAI is its ability to create novel and imaginative content, thus fostering creativity and innovation within the workplace. Creative professionals, including artists, designers, and writers, can harness GenAI as a powerful tool to develop ideas, produce original artwork, and craft engaging content. As GenAI continues to advance, its impact on creativity and productivity in the workplace is set to be even more profound.

GenAI Chatbots

Chatbots are intelligent programs designed to engage users in natural language conversations. They possess the capability to comprehend user input and generate relevant responses. A popular application of chatbots is in providing customer support for companies through their websites. For instance, if a person encounters issues with their cable television, they can visit the provider's website and initiate a conversation with the chatbot to seek solutions to their service problems. These chatbots are engineered to simulate human-like interactions, creating a sense of interaction with a live person.

Beyond customer service, chatbots have expanded their utility to include generating original texts. Among the widely used GenAI chatbots are OpenAI's ChatGPT and Google's Gemini. Both ChatGPT and Gemini effectively respond to prompts and offer users a diverse array of text options. Their advanced capabilities empower users to explore creative content generation through interactive conversations.

The most common uses of chatbots are the following:

Answering questions: Chatbots can answer questions in a comprehensive and informative way to help users learn information quickly and efficiently.

Generating text: Chatbots can generate different creative formats of text content like essays, blog posts, poems, scripts, musical pieces, emails, letters, etc.

Translating languages: Chatbots can translate text into more than 100 languages, allowing users to understand or communicate with a broader audience.

Leveling text: Chatbots can rewrite a text at various reading levels to support diverse learning needs.

Summarizing text: Chatbots can summarize long articles or web pages into a few sentences, allowing users to process information more efficiently.

Brainstorming ideas: Chatbots can help users brainstorm ideas for projects, articles, or blog posts and act as a thought partner to help gain new perspectives.

Writing code: Chatbots can write and debug code in a variety of programming languages to empower coders to be more creative with their applications.

Collaborating: Chatbots can be a sounding board and collaborate on projects by sharing ideas, feedback, and suggestions to ensure clarity in one's writing and ideas.

In schools, these platforms have become indispensable tools supporting academic endeavors. Chatbots play a crucial role in assisting with research, paper writing, presentation creation, and exam preparation. Creative writers also benefit from these platforms, utilizing them to generate ideas, brainstorm plots, and craft compelling dialogues.

Businesses have also recognized the value of GenAI in streamlining various tasks. These chatbots are now integral to customer service, marketing strategies, and product development processes, enhancing overall efficiency and effectiveness. On a personal level, individuals have embraced these tools, employing them for tasks like vacation planning, email composition, and menu and shopping list creation.

As chatbots continue to evolve, their potential for innovative and creative applications will only expand further, and they will undoubtedly become even more ubiquitous.

Generative AI Image Generators

Besides generating text, GenAI has been developed to create images. With some basic prompt engineering and some creativity, even the novice can produce some stunning and imaginative images never seen before. Like its text-based brethren, AI image generators scour the Internet for images, take basic elements from them, and compile them into novel productions.

Text-to-image programs like Dall-E 2, Midjourney, and Imagine AI Art Generator have revolutionized the creative landscape, enabling the rapid generation of unlimited designs. With the help of GenAI, I can effortlessly request the creation of imaginative mashups, like envisioning a flamingo superhero. This technology becomes a potent tool in the hands of students, empowering them to craft distinctive logos, layouts, and visual elements tailored to specific requirements and preferences. Not only does this save valuable time, but it also infuses students with newfound inspiration and novel perspectives, breaking through creative barriers and propelling them to explore uncharted territories.

Created by Aaron Blackwelder via Canva.com

AI art generators hold boundless potential for students to reimagine school mascots, for example, be it for student government, homecoming week, sporting events, band performances, or other activities. Embracing these innovative tools, students can infuse their creativity into various school events, fostering a sense of ownership and uniqueness in every endeavor.

Creativity stands as a cornerstone of twenty-first-century education, and its nourishment thrives on inspiration. GenAI image-creating platforms offer precisely that, infusing students with fresh perspectives and new possibilities. Leveraging the prowess of graphic AI tools like Dall-E 2 and Imagine AI Art Generator, students gain access to powerful algorithms capable of producing unique and unconventional visuals, expanding beyond the boundaries of conventional design. By embracing these platforms, students' creative horizons widen, sparking an influx of innovative ideas and propelling them toward artistic brilliance.

Created by Aaron Blackwelder via Adobe Firefly

GENERATIVE AI IN THE WORKSPACE

Workspace tools such as word processing, presentation software, spreadsheets, and email are getting smarter thanks to AI. This AI infusion aims to streamline workflows and boost efficiency for professionals. Imagine creating documents like proposals or client letters with just a prompt! Presentations can be whipped up in seconds by feeding the AI a topic, data, and desired length. Spreadsheets become more powerful with AI suggesting formulas, analyzing data, and generating visuals automatically. Even emails get a boost, with AI assistants summarizing key points and helping craft responses.

Beyond efficiency, AI in workspaces empowers users. It unlocks a wellspring of knowledge and lets them create content that reflects their unique voice and needs. These tools are designed to be partners, not replacements. As our students enter a workforce that expects them to leverage these AI tools, educators must become familiar with them as well. This will prepare students to thrive in a world where AI assistance is the norm.

GENERATIVE AI FOR EDUCATION

Imagine a classroom where history comes alive through a conversation with Gandhi or a heated debate about literature with Hermione Granger. This isn't science fiction; it's the potential of AI in education.

Using GenAI, teachers can streamline their workload, including lesson planning and differentiation, and spend more time engaging with students in meaningful ways. For example, GenAI can provide basic scores and feedback on student work based on sample rubrics so teachers can focus more deeply on student ideas. Additionally, teachers can allow students to submit assignments to AI chatbots before the assignment is due, to receive immediate and actionable feedback.

Teachers can also leverage AI to support student learning by creating their own interactive learning experiences, even with minimal technical skills. Teachers can design chatbots that act as tutors, historical figures, or even research assistants. This allows for focused learning journeys, guiding students through curated resources, which enables them to delve deeper into class content, sparking curiosity and critical thinking. Debate bots further hone these skills, allowing students to tackle complex topics and prepare for discussions. Q&A bots can even provide students with a safe space to ask questions and receive answers with links to reliable sources.

AI in education isn't a replacement for teachers; it's a powerful tool that strengthens their role. By partnering with AI, teachers can personalize learning, ensure students master key content, and develop critical thinking skills in a way that fosters meaningful interactions and student success.

CONCERNS ABOUT GENERATIVE AI IN EDUCATION

GenAI is changing education. It is understandable to be concerned about how this impacts the critical work of teachers. But it's important to remember as educators, we have survived changes in the past, like the widespread adoption of the Internet or even graphing calculators, so there is no reason to believe that we will not survive this change as well. After all, if there was one thing that became clear during the remote learning phase of the COVID-19 pandemic, it was the importance of the human and relational element of learning. No amount of GenAI will ever be able to provide that. Even still, here are some of the top concerns we hear from educators around the country:

Diminished academic integrity: One of the greatest concerns educators have is academic integrity. How will they know whether students wrote their papers themselves when GenAI can be prompted to write the paper for them? This causes teachers to spend extra time reviewing students' writing and playing gotcha, which costs time and stress for the student and the teacher. Cheating is not a new concern in education. Educators have dealt with cheating for decades: students have copied assignments, found test questions ahead of time, or even gotten someone else to write a paper for them. GenAI allows student writing to be copied as easily as some of the other instances of cheating. One way to get around this is to AI-proof your assignments. This doesn't mean using AI detection software to catch cheating. Instead, rethink the prompts and tasks students are challenged with so that AI cannot answer for the student but might even be able to support the student to complete the tasks more effectively. This will be discussed later in the book.

Reduced effort or critical thinking: Another concern is that student work will no longer require effort or critical thinking. For example, writing is a skill, so part of this worry is that by not practicing the skill (writing) students will not develop into strong writers. Students may ask, "Why bother with writing when I can have a machine do it for me?" When used properly, GenAI should challenge students. Students need to develop complementary skills using AI to draft and refine their ideas. Remember that the skill underlying writing is thinking. GenAI will challenge students to apply more critical thinking, assist them to become more effective and thoughtful communicators, and enable them to see the power of effective communication.

Eventual skill replacement: Some teachers worry that GenAI will make learning some skills such as writing, and even the instruction of those skills in school, obsolete. If the machines can do it better, why bother learning certain academic skills at all? Ultimately, the same argument could be made for math when calculators became ubiquitous. Math instruction has not vanished; it has simply shifted to include thinking and explaining. A basic understanding of essential academic skills is still needed to be effective. GenAI merged with these basic skills will help students thrive.

Potential job displacement: Eventually, there is a worry that even teachers themselves can be replaced by GenAI. If a computer can teach a student the parts of a cell, or how to find the area of a circle, are educators needed? What if this AI can also edit and score student projects? The worry that GenAI can replace teachers is real. However, even if it could do all of those things, online instruction during the pandemic exposed just how valuable in-person, social education is. Because learning is a social act, educators do not have to be worried about being replaced by machines.

Discernment of credible information: Even teachers who want to use GenAI have lots of concerns about the technology itself. Because it tries to sound credible and knowledgeable, GenAI will make up information that sounds plausible even when it is not. This is highly dangerous, especially for students who are just starting to learn about a topic. Students will not necessarily have the expert knowledge to spot false information. Not only that, but it is very easy to have the AI generate plausible information and much harder to have students check the information to make sure it is correct. As we will discuss later in the book, this will require students to learn and practice specific skills related to confirming the accuracy of information.

Knowledge of information bias: AI is only as good as its input, and the training set for our LLM AI tools has been the Internet, which is written by primarily by white, middle-class, and upper-class males (Jesutofunmi et al., 2023). Bias from historical sources can also easily seep in because part of GenAI's job is to sound authentic to the text it is based on, including sharing those perspectives. For example, when ChatGPT is asked what happened on the Oregon Trail, it may respond that the pioneers faced "hostile encounters with Native American tribes" (ChatGPT, May 11, 2024) but make no mention of land that was taken from those tribes. As with the false information concerns above, students need to develop skills around the detection and correction of bias. This concern will be addressed later on in Chapter 4.

Disruption of the status quo: GenAI can change education. The widespread use of AI may disrupt the way students learn and communicate. AI will certainly challenge pedagogy and the way educators operate. Low-level assignments are more susceptible to GenAI. However, educators can partner with students, checking work and asking students to explain the decisions they made during the process of completing the project. This will be further explored in Chapter 5.

HOPES FOR AI IN EDUCATION

Despite these concerns, GenAI has enormous potential. Used properly, GenAI can help reduce inequities inherent in education by reducing the skill gap between the highest- and lowest-performing students. Research supports this both for students in the classroom and workers across a large range of jobs. Professor Ethan Mollick (2023) cites numerous studies across different professions showing that "AI acts as a skills leveler for a huge range of professional work. If you were in the bottom half of the skill distribution for writing, idea generation, analyses, or any of a number of other professional tasks you will likely find that, with the help of AI, you have become quite good." AI has the potential to assist workers and students who have historically found writing and thinking tasks difficult.

This is especially true of writing tasks. Research at MIT by Noy and Zhang (2023) suggests that workers with poor writing ability who use ChatGPT for writing benefit the most. "Inequality between workers decreases, as ChatGPT compresses the productivity distribution by benefiting low-ability workers more." This mirrors some of our personal classroom research discussed in Chapter 3, where the lowest performing group of students demonstrated some of the largest increases in writing scores.

Beyond writing tasks, GenAI can act as a thought partner to help students communicate their ideas effectively. It can tutor students who otherwise would not have access to tutoring outside of school. GenAI can help translate student writing and teacher worksheets more effectively than tools like Google Translate.

GenAI can also help teachers save time by helping them plan units, come up with lists of vocabulary words, draft emails, rewrite assignments, and much more. Also, the more knowledgeable the teacher is about a topic, the better they will be able to prompt the AI to generate useful outputs.

Ultimately, students need to be ready for the world that awaits them after high school. Workers from every industry imaginable are using these tools. We need to prepare our students for a future in which they will be expected to use GenAI effectively, and that means using it in our classrooms.

CHAPTER REVIEW

The Big Ideas

Chapter 1 discussed both the benefits and drawbacks of generative AI in education. It emphasized the importance of using generative AI responsibly and effectively to improve learning outcomes and included the following:

- **What is generative AI?** Generative AI is a type of artificial intelligence that is trained to generate creative text formats, like poems, code, scripts, musical pieces, etc. It works by recognizing patterns and predicting what the likeliest response would be to a prompt.

- **How generative AI works:** Large Language Models (LLMs) are generative AI systems trained on massive amounts of text data. They can answer your questions in a comprehensive and informative way, generate different creative text formats, translate languages, summarize text, brainstorm ideas, and even write code.

- **How generative AI is used:** Generative AI is being integrated into various tools and platforms like search engines, social media, and workspace software. It can streamline tasks such as writing emails, creating presentations, and generating creative content.

- **Student use of generative AI:** In education, generative AI can be used to help students as a writing assistant, supporting brainstorming ideas, plot development, and crafting dialogues. Generative AI also has the potential to reduce inequities among students by providing free or inexpensive tutoring and making education more accessible for diverse learners.

- **Teacher use of generative AI:** Teachers can use generative AI to create quizzes and assessments, differentiate lesson plans, and change the reading level of a piece of text. It can also help teachers save time and improve their productivity.

- **Concerns about generative AI:** Concerns about the use of generative AI in education include diminished academic integrity, reduced student effort, and potential job replacement for teachers.

You Try It: Generating Writing Prompts With Large Language Models (LLMs)

Use a large language model (LLM) like ChatGPT or Google Gemini to brainstorm "bell ringer" writing prompts for students.

What You'll Need:

- Access to a computer with Internet connection

- An account with a Large Language Model (LLM) platform such as the following (other LLMs might be available depending on your region and preferences):
  - ChatGPT (https://openai.com/chatgpt)
  - Google Gemini (https://gemini.google.com)

Instructions:

1. Choose your LLM platform and create an account (if needed) or log in to your existing account.

2. Decide on the type of writing prompt you want to generate. Think about the writing skills you want your students to practice, the genre you're focusing on, or the theme you'd like to explore. Here are some examples:
   - Process prompts: Explain an experiment, how to solve a mathematical equation, or the process for a bill to become a law.
   - Narrative prompts: Generate a story starter with a specific setting (e.g., a futuristic city on Mars), a character description (e.g., a robot with a secret), or a conflict (e.g., a missing object with magical powers).
   - Descriptive prompts: Describe a character, a place, or an object in detail, using all five senses.

(Continued)

(Continued)

- Argument prompts: Write a persuasive essay on a controversial topic (e.g., Should schools have uniforms?).
- Poetic prompts: Generate a poem with a specific rhyme scheme or meter or based on a particular image or emotion.

3. Craft your prompt for the LLM. Be clear and specific about what you want the LLM to generate. Here are some tips:
   - Start with a clear instruction. For example, "Generate creative writing prompts for bell ringer activities."
   - Provide additional details if needed. For example, "Students are currently learning about mitosis."
   - Consider the age and skill level of your students. For example, "Design this for multiple abilities and provide differentiated options."

4. Input your prompt into the LLM platform. Follow the platform's instructions on how to submit your prompt.

5. Generate and review the prompts. The LLM will generate one or more writing prompts based on your input. Review the prompts and choose the ones that are most appropriate for your students' needs.

Additional Tips:

- You can experiment with different prompts and refine them based on the results you get.
- Consider using the generated prompts as a starting point and then adding your own creative twist to them.
- Discuss the generated prompts with your students and have them explain why they find them interesting or challenging.

Questions for Reflection

1. Which concern about generative AI in education worries you the most? Why?

2. What aspect of using generative AI in education are you most excited about?

3. Is there a risk that AI could become another burden on teachers, requiring them to learn new skills and navigate complex software? Explain your thoughts.

4. After reading Chapter 1, what new ideas or possibilities do you see for using generative AI in your classroom?

Follow the link or scan the QR code for more helpful resources related to the content found in Chapter 1.

EMPOWERING EDUCATORS IN THE AGE OF AI

A Message From Aaron

I received an email from an English teacher named Naomi at an alternative high school in my district. Naomi works hard to meet the diverse learning needs of her students who range from ninth through twelfth grade. She spends hours after school and over the weekend preparing differentiated materials to meet her students' unique interests and learning needs. She knew I had experience with AI tools and wanted to learn how she could use them to help her better support her students, many of whom struggle to meet grade-level proficiency in reading and writing.

Naomi is a passionate teacher who previously taught special education. She understands the need to differentiate in order to engage students and promote learning. Her students are ages 14 through 21 and want to earn a high school diploma, but they all have major hurdles that make attending a traditional comprehensive high school difficult. Some struggle with anxiety and being in large crowds, causing them overwhelming stress. Others come from homes where they need to take care of siblings or they need to work to help support their families. She also has two students who are parents and plan to get married after they graduate high school. Both want to earn their diploma to establish a foundation that will support their relationship and model the importance of education for their child. Her students range in ability—some read at a second-grade level and others are at or above their enrolled

(Continued)

(Continued)

grade level. She wants to help her students and does all she can to create material that caters to their individual needs. But with such a wide range of social, learning, and academic student needs, Naomi is exhausted.

I sat down with Naomi and showed her how AI can help her meet the needs of her students while giving her back her free time. I showed her how it can be used as a research assistant, helping students find pertinent information quickly and efficiently to better support research projects. I showed her how it can rewrite texts to support student reading levels so all students can engage with the essential content. I showed her how AI enables her to create lessons, generate differentiated learning supports, provide students with actionable feedback, and generate rubrics. She now has access to tools that enable her to meet the needs of her diverse learners and recapture her personal time. As I showed her these tools, I could feel her burden leave the room. Naomi cried and said, "This allows me to do my job."

Whenever I show teachers how AI can help them, I am met with relief and gratitude. Teachers want to be able to engage their students and support each of them to be successful. Before the advent of AI, it meant either teachers spent their evenings and weekends doing planning and preparing or they gave up and accepted the idea that not all students would have their needs met. With the support of AI, teachers can, in a matter of seconds, generate materials that can challenge and engage students through personalized learning.

Aaron

Imagine being told you have to teach a unit you have never taught before. You don't have a teacher's guide, though you can spend time scrolling through random plans online. Your coworkers are helpful, but they're too overwhelmed themselves to sit with you and talk you through the new unit. One of them shares his Google Drive for the unit with you, which contains ten years' worth of worksheets and tests but no context. Many teachers have probably lived this experience before. GenAI can change all that by helping teachers plan, revise, and scaffold the units they teach.

It's easy to think about the impact of GenAI from a student's point of view; they will be aided immensely. However, GenAI tools have the potential to help teachers as much or more than students. GenAI can help plan units, create worksheets, create exemplars, and even differentiate text. GenAI can also help revise teacher-created work and flat-out save time. It can be a potent thought partner for brainstorming ideas, help writing newsletters, and can even be used as a sounding board when having to send out a difficult email. Educators' workflows have changed at almost every level. Ultimately, GenAI allows more customization of content and enables educators to support students better with the time they have available.

LESSON AND UNIT PLANNING

Lesson planning is one of the most straightforward uses of GenAI. Teachers can write lessons and units as well as generate draft assignments based on those units. For example, if a teacher wanted to develop a unit on something they hadn't taught before, like a unit on microorganisms, the Civil Rights era, or the play *MacBeth*, they could ask GenAI to come up with a unit plan for their grade level. It is the teacher's responsibility to ensure that the materials generated by AI are appropriate for students and still meet the required learning targets. Even still, in less than a minute a draft roadmap is made available. It takes much less time to look at a draft plan and revise it than it does to come up with something from scratch. In the age of AI, GenAI will help streamline the lesson planning process. The hours spent trudging through Google or scrolling through paid peer-to-peer lesson-sharing platforms can be a thing of the past.

Feeding unit ideas into GenAI is very fast and infinitely customizable. Most importantly, these units will still be based on the ideas and existing units a teacher puts into GenAI. This will help teachers save time and mental energy.

Alternatively, a teacher may have a lesson or unit that needs content revised or added to it because it is lacking rigor on a specific learning objective. Teachers can use GenAI to modify their existing content or prompt it to create new content to fill in the gaps. Here are some ideas:

- Brainstorm cause and effect writing prompts

- Draft rubrics or scoring guides for current assignments

- Modify existing rubrics and scoring guides

- Create exemplars based on existing rubrics and scoring guides

Remember, the teacher is the expert in the room, so everything GenAI is used for should be checked and revised. AI can save time by doing 80% of the work for the teacher. This frees the teacher to focus on the remaining 20%, which includes critical analysis and reflection. Figure 2.1 is a sample lesson designed using a chatbot.

CHATbot

Design an introductory lesson plan to orient 7th graders to the concept of rational numbers.

Lesson Title: Cracking the Code: Unveiling Rational Numbers
Grade Level: 7th
Subject: Math
Time Allotment: 60 minutes
Learning Objectives:

- Students will be able to define rational numbers.
- Students will be able to identify different representations of rational numbers (fractions, decimals, integers).
- Students will be able to classify a number as rational or irrational (basic understanding).

Materials:

- Whiteboard or projector
- Markers/pens
- Chart paper
- Fraction manipulatives (optional)
- Decimal manipulatives (optional)
- Worksheet with various numbers (including fractions, decimals, and integers)

Lesson Procedure:
Introduction (10 minutes):

1. **Warm-Up (5 minutes):** Play a quick game of "Number Line Showdown." Divide the class into two teams and project a blank number line on the board. Call out numbers (positive and negative integers, fractions) and have students from each team race to mark the number on the line correctly. Briefly discuss how some numbers are easy to place and some might be trickier.
2. **Hook (5 minutes):** Present a real-life scenario: "Imagine you want to share a pizza equally with 3 friends. How much pizza does each person get?" After students answer (1/4), introduce the concept of fractions and how they represent parts of a whole.

Activity (25 minutes):

1. **Building the Definition (10 minutes):** Divide students into small groups and provide manipulatives (fraction strips...

· · ·

Enter your prompt here.

Created by Aaron Blackwelder via Canva.com

GENERATING VOCABULARY CONTENT

Vocabulary instruction is another example where GenAI shines. It can create customized vocabulary lists for any text, whether it is a small news article or a large unit. If a teacher wants to teach tenth graders a unit on the impact of human activity on biodiversity, for example, they can ask GenAI to suggest a list of key terms students should know and understand. As a content area expert, the teacher would then revise that initial list as needed. GenAI can even look at a current news article and generate a list of vocabulary words from that text.

GenAI allows teachers to implement as much vocabulary as they desire in their units. A teacher can then prompt GenAI to use those vocabulary lists in worksheets, assessments, and projects it is asked to create. In doing this, teachers can ensure that students will consistently see these vocabulary words. Students will receive lots of practice with the terms as they move through a unit, focusing and reinforcing the vocabulary they have been taught. This also helps ensure that students see the words being used correctly in context with minimal teacher effort. See Figure 2.2 for a sample vocabulary list generated by a chatbot.

GENERATING QUESTIONS ABOUT A TEXT

Designing comprehension and discussion questions can be challenging and time consuming. It takes thought and effort to create a variety of questions that are accessible to the students as well as address the necessary standards and learning objectives. Instead of spending time doing this yourself, GenAI can easily create questions about a text. The teacher can feed an article into GenAI and ask it to create comprehension questions. GenAI can also generate open-ended discussion questions. This can be a powerful tool for Socratic seminars, for example. When the goal is to engage students in discussion and thinking about a text, GenAI can help write the questions. Teachers can also set up chatbots to help students in the creation of effective discussion questions. Figure 2.3 is a sample set of comprehension and discussion questions generated by a chatbot from a text about the Inca Empire.

CHANGING TYPES AND FORMS OF QUESTIONS

Another possible use for GenAI is to change the complexity and type of the questions. For example, students who struggle with reading comprehension can be provided with basic comprehension questions. Short-answer questions could even be rewritten as multiple-choice questions. On the other hand, students who need more challenging tasks can be provided with more complex open-ended questions.

CHATbot

Hello CHATbot. Please create a vocabulary list of key terms to understand mitosis for a 7th grade science class.

Key Vocabulary for Understanding Mitosis:
- **Cell**: The basic unit of life, like a tiny building block that makes up all living **things**.
- **Cell Division**: The process where a single cell makes two new identical cells.
- **Mitosis**: A specific type of cell division that creates two daughter cells with the same number of chromosomes as the parent cell.
- **Chromosomes**: Thread-like structures in the cell that carry genetic information (like instructions). Imagine them as the blueprints for building an organism.
- **DNA** (Deoxyribonucleic Acid): The molecule that makes up chromosomes and contains the instructions for building an organism. Think of DNA as the code written on the blueprints.
- **Chromatid**: Each chromosome is copied before cell division, resulting in two sister chromatids joined at a central point. Imagine copying the blueprints and having two identical copies temporarily attached.
- **Centromere**: The central point where sister chromatids are attached.
- **Nucleus**: The control center of the cell where chromosomes are found. Think of it as the office where the blueprints are stored.
- **Cytoplasm**: The jelly-like material inside the cell outside the nucleus. Imagine it as all the building materials and tools needed to follow the blueprints.
- **Cell Membrane**: The outer boundary of the cell that controls what enters and leaves. Think of it as a security gate around the building site.
- **Interphase**: The "growing" stage of the cell cycle where the cell prepares for division by copying its DNA and organelles. This is like gathering all the materials and workers before construction begins.
- **Mitosis** (Phases):
- **Prophase**: Chromosomes condense and become visible. The blueprints are unfolded and reviewed.

Enter your prompt here.

Created by Aaron Blackwelder via Canva.com

CHATbot

Hi CHATbot, can you generate 5 comprehension questions and 5 discussion questions for 6th grade students about the following article?

Comprehension Questions (6th Grade):
1. What was the name of the Inca Empire's government?
2. How many quarters (suyu) did the Inca Empire divide their land into?
3. What was the smallest unit of government in the Inca Empire called?
4. What were two ways the Inca collected taxes?
5. What was the name of the Inca god of the Sun?

Discussion Questions (6th Grade):
1. Why do you think the Inca Empire needed a complex government structure?
2. Imagine you are a young person living in the Inca Empire. Would you prefer to live in a large city like Cuzco or a smaller village? Why?
3. The article mentions the Inca had a system of roads, but commoners were not allowed to use them. Do you think this was a fair rule? Why or why not?
4. The Inca achieved many things without technologies we consider important today, like the wheel or writing. What does this tell you about human ingenuity?
5. The Inca religion included sacrifices. How does this practice compare to religious practices in your own culture?

Enter your prompt here.

Created by Aaron Blackwelder via Canva.com

When using GenAI to write or rewrite questions it is always important to check the output before placing these questions in front of students. Multiple-choice questions seem especially variable. However, revising test questions is much quicker than coming up with new questions entirely.

To demonstrate question conversions, a chatbot was asked to rewrite a question about *To Kill a Mockingbird* first as a multiple-choice question. Then the chatbot was asked to rewrite the question using every level of Bloom's Taxonomy. See the chat in Figure 2.4.

CHATbot

Hi CHATbot, Can you rewrite the following questions first into a multiple choice question and then questions that reflect every level of Bloom's Taxonomy:

What is Atticus's advice to Scout about school/learning to get along with people?

Of course! Here is the question rewritten in multiple choice:
What is Atticus's advice to Scout about school/learning to get along with people?
    a. "Never judge a book by its cover."
    b. "Treat others how you want to be treated."
    c. "Always be the smartest person in the room."
    d. "Avoid making friends to avoid complications."

Here is the question rewritten at different levels of Bloom's Taxonomy:
- Remember:
  - What is Atticus's advice to Scout about school, learning, and getting along with people?
- Understand:
  - Summarize Atticus's guidance to Scout regarding school and interpersonal relationships.
- Apply:
  - How might Scout implement Atticus's advice in her daily interactions at school?
- Analyze:
  - Break down Atticus's advice, examining its components. How might each aspect contribute to Scout's development?
- Evaluate:
  - Assess the effectiveness of Atticus's advice. Are there situations where it might not be applicable or could be improved?
- Create:
  - Devise a piece of advice that aligns with Atticus's principles but addresses a different aspect of Scout's school life or relationships.

Enter your prompt here.

Created by Aaron Blackwelder via Canva.com

These questions ask students to demonstrate the same basic knowledge of the text; therefore, the same content and understanding can be assessed using different types of questions. The questions can be more accessible or more challenging depending on the needs of the students.

Separate versions of tests can also be created easily. In years past, educators who needed different versions of a test sometimes had to use tests that asked about different things. Using GenAI to rewrite questions ensures that each version of the test will be asking questions about the same things.

GenAI can also turn multiple-choice questions into short-answer questions. This is more effective than simply turning regular questions into multiple-choice questions, as short-answer questions require more critical thinking from students. Educators could use this method to turn a test into a review for students. Imagine taking a multiple-choice test, asking GenAI to reword those questions as short-answer questions, and then using those short-answer questions as a way to help students review for an upcoming test. This can be done in seconds using GenAI tools.

TEACHING CONTENT AND SKILLS IN DIFFERENT WAYS

Teachers often recycle the same units for many years. It is easy to get stuck when this happens. Over time, standards, students, and pedagogy evolve and teachers need to evolve as well. GenAI can help keep units up to date and focused on the needs of current students. For example, a teacher can ask it to take a prompt they have written and then incorporate or focus on new standards. GenAI can also provide ideas for adapting old units to the current standards and skills, making the lesson more relevant. It can even help teachers collaborate to align their units to promote fidelity within a department.

A second way to refresh units is to ask GenAI to change what students are asked to produce, such as changing from an essay to a podcast. A presentation about childhood development might be turned into a case study, a timeline, or a series of letters to children at different ages. GenAI can offer multiple options, such as writing a movie script, generating an infographic, or creating a presentation. If educators want to teach similar content or skills differently, they can keep the general expectations of the project intact but update or refresh the student output.

Figure 2.5 is a sample prompt from a chatbot suggesting new student products for a teacher's existing health unit.

CHATbot

Hi CHATbot, here is a 9th grade health presentation I have used in the past. I would like to teach the same concepts in a different way. Can you look at these directions and give me other ways to teach the same content?

Absolutely! Here are some alternative ways to teach the same concepts about childhood development for your 9th-grade health class:

1. Interactive Activities:

- Growth Stages Relay Race: Divide students into teams, each representing a stage of childhood (Early, Middle, Late). At each station, students complete a task related to the stage's development (e.g., building blocks for early childhood motor skills, writing a persuasive letter for middle childhood social development). The first team to finish represents how children progress through these stages.
- "Dear Younger Me" Letters: Have students write letters to their younger selves, reflecting on the physical, social, and emotional changes they've experienced. This can be a great way to spark self-awareness and solidify their understanding of childhood development.

2. Project-Based Learning:

- Childhood Timeline: Have students create a timeline of their own lives, highlighting key milestones and changes in physical, social, and emotional development.
- "Child Development Through the Decades" Presentations: Divide students into groups, each assigned a different decade (e.g., 1980s, 1990s). They research and present on how childhood experiences, toys, and societal expectations differed across these periods.

3. Technology Integration:

- Create a Class Blog: Have students can take turns posting articles on various aspects of childhood development. This encourages research, writing skills, and peer learning.
- "Growing Up" Documentary Project: Have students research and create short documentaries focused on specific aspects of childhood development (e.g., brain development, and social pressures in different cultures).

These are just a few ideas to get you started. Remember to tailor the activities and level of complexity to your students' interests and learning styles.

Enter your prompt here.

Created by Aaron Blackwelder via Canva.com

DIFFERENTIATING READING MATERIALS

It is not uncommon to teach students with IEPs and advanced students in the same classroom. These students require texts at different reading levels than their peers. It is likely that even without considering those two identified groups of students, the range of reading needs is far wider in classrooms today than teachers experienced in years past, especially for those who taught before the COVID-19 pandemic, as reading scores have consistently dropped since the pandemic (Walton, 2023). Finding differentiated text to support these students requires extra work. This can apply to assignments as well. Fortunately, GenAI can be used to rewrite tasks, directions, and even whole pieces of text at different reading levels or in multiple languages to support diverse learners.

If a teacher wants to provide their ninth-grade English class with a short biography of William Shakespeare, for example, they can also have ChatGPT rewrite that biography at various grade reading levels to meet the needs of students. Additionally, it can rewrite questions about that article at a different grade reading level or generate questions based on the new version(s) of the text it created. GenAI can do this in a matter of minutes.

Remember, when using GenAI, it is important to check to make sure the outputs are appropriate for the task and audience. One thing to be aware of is that the AI's idea of a certain grade's reading level may differ from the teacher's idea of appropriate grade-level text. When GenAI is used in this fashion, users can ask it to rewrite a text at a few different grade levels to see whether its reading levels correspond with their own.

This has been mentioned elsewhere, but text can also be translated into other languages. In practice, it seems to do a better job than Google Translate. This will help support students who are learning English.

GENERATING STUDENT EXEMPLARS

An exemplar is a sample of work demonstrating high quality in a particular subject or skill. It could be an exemplary essay, a well-executed science experiment, a skillful artwork, or any other product demonstrating a high proficiency or understanding. Teachers use exemplars to help students understand what is expected of them and to provide them with a model to emulate.

Exemplars can be helpful for students in the following ways:

- **Help students understand success criteria for a given task.** When students see exemplars, they see high-quality work. This can help them to focus their efforts and to make sure that they are meeting the standards.

- **Provide students with a model to emulate.** Exemplars can show students what good work looks like. This can help them to develop their skills and to improve their work.

- **Encourage self-assessment.** When students see exemplars, they can compare their work to the exemplar. This can help them identify strengths and weaknesses in their own work and make improvement plans.

- **Promote peer assessment.** Students can use the exemplars to help practice providing peer feedback. This can help students learn from each other and improve their work.

- **Build personal confidence.** When students have a clear vision of what success looks like, they are more likely to feel confident in their abilities. Exemplars can boost students' self-assurance, as they see that excellence is attainable.

- **Respect different learning styles.** Exemplars cater to various learning styles. Visual learners benefit from seeing exemplary artwork, while auditory learners may gain insights from listening to an exemplary speech or presentation.

Exemplars are valuable tools that facilitate learning, help students improve their skills, and promote a deeper understanding of subject matter across various educational disciplines.

Hawe and Dixon (2023) suggest "exemplars act as a form of inspiration, helping students to get started and to structure their work. It does not affect their ability to produce original, creative, and high-quality work—in fact, exemplars can increase student self-efficacy and can give them the confidence to do better."

However, creating exemplars is time consuming. Educators teaching a new unit may need access to high-quality exemplars to help support their students. Coming up with exemplars can take hours or days to complete. This means teachers spend personal time creating exemplars or simply do not make them.

With the help of AI, teachers can create exemplars quickly and easily that will help support student success. To do this, a teacher would copy and paste the content of a rubric into the prompt and ask AI to provide exemplars that would meet all the provided criteria. Teachers can even request multiple examples by writing a prompt that asks, "Provide three (or more) examples demonstrating work that meets the expectations of this rubric."

If the teacher is not satisfied with the exemplar provided, they can simply ask AI to make modifications. For example, ask it to rewrite the exemplar

- citing specific sources.

- including certain facts or data points.

- with more detail.

- highlighting a specific point.

- at a different reading level.

- for non-examples that may include errors.

Exemplars are a valuable tool for both teachers and students. When used effectively, exemplars can help students to understand the standards, develop skills, and improve student work. Here are some additional tips to consider when creating AI-generated exemplars for the classroom:

- Make sure the exemplars are relevant to the learning goals.

- Create exemplars that represent various levels of achievement.

- Provide students with opportunities to discuss the exemplars and to identify the criteria for success.

- Use exemplars to facilitate peer assessment.

FACILITATING COMMUNICATION

Parent communication is essential for teachers to be able to provide students with the best possible education. By communicating regularly with parents, teachers can build strong partnerships, address educational concerns, and help parents understand ways to be involved in their children's education.

Parents want to partner with teachers to support their child's education. According to Samantha Arce (2019, p. 91), parents want more frequent communication about their child's behavior and academics and more opportunities to learn how to help their child succeed academically. GenAI can help streamline this communication and provoke more parent engagement.

John Hattie's research suggests parental involvement has an effective size of 0.51. With a "hinge-point" of 0.40 (the point in which a category demonstrates a desired effectiveness), engaging parents in a child's education makes a positive impact (Constantino, 2016). When teachers communicate regularly with parents, they can build a strong partnership based on trust and respect. This partnership can help ensure that parents are involved in their children's education and work with teachers to support student learning. One way teachers can promote involvement is through weekly newsletters or emails.

Newsletters

One of the most effective ways teachers can communicate with families is through a regular (e.g., weekly) newsletter. Newsletters help inform parents and guardians about projects, essential learning, and school activities. However, creating regular newsletters can become time-consuming and teachers can get writer's block, making it easy to get off track when things get busy or new ideas don't flow.

AI can be an excellent partner to help support teachers as they create their newsletters. A teacher may know what they want to share with student families, but finding the time and creativity can be difficult. Prompting AI to write a newsletter can simplify the task and ensure families are receiving important information that can help them support their child's learning. See Figure 2.6 for an example newsletter.

CHATbot

Hi CHATbot, Write a newsletter for a mathematics classroom to send to parents. This week we are covering finding the area of a circle and this is Pi week so bring pies by Friday for a class activity.

Hello Parents,
This week in math class, we're getting our slice of pi(e)!
We'll be diving into the world of circles, learning how to find their area.
Circles are everywhere – from pizzas to frisbees, coins to clocks!
Here's a sneak peek at what your child will be learning:
- What is the area?
- Understanding pi (π) and its role in circles.
- Using the formula for finding the area of a circle (πr^2).
- Applying this knowledge to solve real-life problems.

Make Math a Slice of Fun: Pi Week Celebration!
To celebrate everyone's favorite mathematical constant (pi, approximately equal to 3.14), we'll be having a fun activity in class this Friday.
We'd love for your child to bring in a pie to share with the class. This will be a delicious way to explore circles and practice our newfound area skills!
Looking for Resources?
Here are some fun online resources to explore circles and pi with your child:
- <u>Circle Song</u> (A catchy song about circles)
- What is Pi? (A short video explaining pi)
- <u>Fun Facts about Pi</u> (Did you know pi has been calculated to trillions of digits?)

We're looking forward to a week of mathematical exploration and a delicious Pi Week celebration!
Happy Learning,
[Your Name]
Math Teacher

Enter your prompt here.

Created by Aaron Blackwelder via Canva.com

There are times when teachers need to communicate with individual parents and guardians to discuss behavior and student progress, schedule meetings, and so on. Emails must get to the point quickly while at the same time demonstrating concern and respect for both student and parent. This can be difficult.

AI can be a sounding board for parent communication. Teachers can write the email and then ask AI what concerns or misconceptions might arise from the way they crafted the email message. It can also suggest tone to help ensure positive parent reception. The teacher can revise the message based on some of the ideas provided by AI.

AI can also help write emails. The teacher can simply ask AI to write an email to a parent about a student's progress in mathematics. Teachers can provide crucial details in the prompt such as the number of missing assignments, when and where students can receive teacher support, and ways in which the parent can help support the student. Doing so will ensure the AI-generated email communicates concerns and solutions to help focus the conversation.

When a teacher wants to share about an upcoming event, such as a performance or field trip, they can ask AI what concerns or frequently asked questions parents might have about the event. AI can generate a list of these questions and the teacher can answer them in the email. This can better inform parents and help reduce the number of follow-up emails asking questions about the event.

Sometimes teachers have to write difficult emails. AI can help write emails that address sensitive behaviors such as students making racist, homophobic, ableist, or other derogatory remarks. AI can provide helpful language that teachers can use to write emails on such sensitive content. For example, if a student makes a racist comment, the teacher can ask AI to help write the email in a sensitive way that addresses the concern in a clear and constructive way without causing harm or shame or using language that could cause the family to become defensive. This can help foster positive communication even about difficult topics.

ALLOWING TEACHERS TO TEACH

AI equips teachers with tools to address the needs of diverse classrooms, such as translation, leveling, and personalization, enabling them to effectively support every student. By reducing teachers' workloads, AI helps them reclaim some of their personal time. With teacher turnover rates at 16% and more than two-thirds leaving before retirement, burnout is cited as the main reason teachers leave the profession (University of Massachusetts Global, n.d.).

Teachers require proper training, support, and resources to perform their jobs well. AI can help alleviate some of the stress by taking over routine tasks, allowing teachers to focus on more meaningful and fulfilling aspects of teaching, like building relationships and challenging students at their level.

Additionally, AI enhances teachers' communication and assessment capabilities, providing meaningful feedback on student learning and writing narratives about student growth. Further discussion on AI's role in assessment will be covered in Chapter 5.

CHAPTER REVIEW

The Big Ideas

Chapter 2 discussed the ways GenAI can help teachers save time and effort while improving the quality of their lessons and communication:

- **Lesson planning:** GenAI can help teachers plan lessons and units, including generating draft assignments and customizing content. It can also streamline the process by eliminating the need to search through online resources.

- **Vocabulary instruction:** GenAI can create vocabulary lists for any text and suggest ways to integrate them into lessons.

- **Question generation:** GenAI can generate comprehension, open-ended, and discussion questions about a text, saving teachers time and effort.

- **Differentiation:** GenAI can differentiate materials for students with different reading levels and needs by rewriting assignments and questions.

- **Assessment:** GenAI can help with assessment by changing the complexity and type of questions, rewriting questions at different levels of Bloom's Taxonomy, and generating exemplars.

- **Exemplar creation:** GenAI can create exemplars (models of high-quality work) to help students understand expectations and improve their work.

- **Communication:** GenAI can help teachers with communication by writing newsletters and emails to parents, suggesting tone, and addressing potential concerns.

You Try It: Use GenAI to Help Create Classroom Content

What You'll Need:

- Access to GenAI such as ChatGPT or Gemini.

1. Think about an upcoming lesson or unit you are teaching. The chart below offers many prompts you can use with GenAI to help create content for your classroom. This includes things like planning lessons and units and building worksheets, tests, and test review materials.

2. Use some of the prompts in Table 2.1 to help you differentiate your lessons or even your explanations to help diverse learners. Adjusting for your own content area, try two of the prompts below.

TABLE 2.1   CHEAT SHEET: EASY PROMPTS FOR GenAI

Generate a list of high-frequency vocabulary words used in this article.	Help plan a unit on mitosis and include the NGSS standards that align with this unit.
Rewrite this biography at a sixth-grade reading level.	Come up with a list of common misconceptions students may have about *Romeo and Juliet.*
Add the following vocabulary words to this assignment.	Come up with three different explanations of how to find the area of a circle for a student who is struggling.
Brainstorm five different ways students can practice using fractions.	Turn this multiple-choice quiz into a study guide for students. Make each question a short-answer question.
Give me ideas on ways to add argumentative writing in my unit about the Oregon Trail.	Write a rubric for an essay based on the following prompt.
Come up with three math story problems based on solving for x.	Write a story using the following vocabulary words in context: appeasement, colonialism, territory, tariff. Write comprehension questions for this text that tie into the vocabulary words.
Write ten comprehension questions based on this article. Include an answer key.	Rewrite this essay prompt to ask students to make a slideshow presentation instead.
Summarize this text.	Rewrite these questions as multiple-choice questions.
Rewrite these questions to make them easier to understand for a student who is struggling.	Write five open-ended discussion questions based on this article.
Rewrite these directions to explain them differently.	Translate this assignment into Spanish.

(Continued)

(Continued)

Questions for Reflection

1. Imagine a student struggling to grasp an important subject in your class. How can GenAI help you provide additional support for this student?

2. Think about the communication methods you use in your classroom. How could you use GenAI to either enhance or streamline communication? What other ideas do you have for using GenAI to improve communication in your classroom?

3. Think about an upcoming unit of instruction. What are some ways GenAI could be used to facilitate collaboration between you and your colleagues? How could GenAI enhance the content being taught?

4. Do you think GenAI will stifle teacher creativity, or can it be used to enhance it? How?

www.beyondthe curriculum.net/ book-1/chapter-2

Follow the link or scan the QR code for more helpful resources related to the content found in Chapter 2.

STUDENT LEARNING IN THE AGE OF AI

A Message From Jason

I had a student, Alan, who was a wonderfully intelligent and thoughtful young man. He had deep interests, and when I asked him to write about those interests, I would receive pages of writing beyond the expected length. The challenge for Alan was that his writing lacked focus and organization. For example, an essay on why virtual reality was the best form of entertainment turned into a three-page article about the history of virtual reality with random arguments along the way.

Alan's writing also lacked internal coherence. Paragraphs seemed random, with no transitions or topic sentences. His writing jumped from place to place. An idea that he mentioned on one page would suddenly pop up several pages later. He struggled to develop his ideas cohesively.

To revise his writing, Alan worked hard, Alan's incredibly supportive parents worked hard, and I worked hard looking at revisions and offering further guidance. By the end of the first semester, Alan was passing English, but everyone involved was feeling a little burnt out. Our collaborative efforts were not sustainable.

When the second semester started, I began experimenting with how ChatGPT could improve student writing. Alan was part of the classroom research that you will see later in this chapter. He was a major beneficiary of ChatGPT.

Alan had the thinking down, but he struggled to organize his thoughts well. He felt frustrated when others had him remove information and ideas to organize his writing. When I showed Alan how

(Continued)

(Continued)

to use ChatGPT to draft writing based on his outlines, he took to it like a fish to water. Alan's average writing scores moved from 2s (approaches standard) to 4s (exceeds standards). Without putting words into their mouth, GenAI empowers students to express their thinking. It is a tool that helps students like Alan succeed in writing, which gave him the confidence he needed to thrive in school.

Jason

As is often the case with new technologies, students are likely to adopt GenAI tools before most of their teachers do. There are many powerful ways students can use GenAI to benefit their own learning. Students can personalize their learning through adaptive platforms offering feedback based on individual needs. These tools can also enhance engagement and understanding by providing content that is targeted at students' interest and abilities. Finally, GenAI can offer accessibility through language translation, text leveling, and alternative modes that help promote a more inclusive learning environment. This chapter will explore ways teachers can leverage GenAI to increase student learning.

GENERATING WRITING FROM STUDENT INPUT

Students are asked to perform various writing tasks across the curriculum. In science, students are tasked to write lab reports, reflections, and even research papers. In social studies, students write historical reports, biographies, and reflections on historical events. In language arts, students write poetry, narratives, speeches, and more. In math, students write proofs and construct arguments or explain their mathematical thinking. Writing is important in school as it helps solidify students' understanding of concepts and helps them develop their voice as a community member.

If the purpose of writing is to communicate ideas, then the process of coming up with the ideas and then publishing those ideas are the essential parts of writing. The construction of sentences, though, is an important skill that often stifles developing writers. Teachers of writing see how the blank page can become a roadblock for many students. Students have the ideas, but they are uncertain how to put them into written words. GenAI can be a support to help students get their ideas on paper.

After pre-writing (research, brainstorming, outlining, etc.), students can take their content and engineer a prompt that helps them bring their ideas to fruition. For example, they could ask GenAI to write a paper and then tell it to include specific details, cite specific sources, and use their outline to ensure the output accurately communicates the student's understanding of the topic.

Learning to write effective prompts is essential, as it differentiates between novel products based on the ideas of the student and generic GenAI writing. Students can further personalize the AI-generated writing by including the following:

- the audience: high school students, newspaper readers, a school board

- genre: argumentative, expository, narrative

- voice: serious, whimsical, humorous

This ensures the piece is written to reflect the uniqueness of the student and the dynamic ways they want to communicate their ideas.

The advent of GenAI helps students share their voices in ways that can instill confidence. If the output reflects the students' thoughts and understanding of a given topic, then the writing truly belongs to the student. Teachers often provide sentence stems and graphic organizers to help students shape their ideas into sentences and paragraphs. The only difference between using a set of teacher-generated sentence stems and graphic organizers and using GenAI is the uniqueness of the students' texts. The essays using teacher-generated tools will read the same, whereas those generated by GenAI will be unique and include more diverse word choices and structures. Reading student work that relies on the same stems over and over becomes monotonous. But when students use GenAI to help generate writing, each piece is unique, especially when students spend time writing dynamic prompts and take the time to critically review the generated texts. Students can learn to develop their voice by revising and editing AI-generated content to communicate their unique ideas. This idea will be further developed in Chapter 5.

Once students have created a piece of writing, they can also use GenAI to focus on different aspects of the text by asking it to generate new versions of the text with a specific purpose in mind. For example, students can examine how word choice impacts the overall tone and message of a text to meet the audience and purpose. Or, students can ask GenAI to rewrite their text in either a formal, whimsical, humorous, or sarcastic tone to help them develop their voice. Not only can it help students write their first draft, but GenAI can also produce multiple drafts and students can find a draft that best suits their needs.

Alternatively, they can select sections from the different drafts to help them compile a draft that best communicates their intent. Google Gemini includes a "View other drafts" option and it defaults to three different drafts. If the draft options are not to the student's liking, they can refresh the response and get three more drafts. In ChatGPT, the user can press the "Regenerate" button as many times as they want to receive a new version of the text. Challenging students to do this helps them become critical thinkers and allows them to learn from multiple drafts to help them develop their voices as writers. Students get the opportunity to see multiple versions of the same piece of writing and learn how words, phrasing, and structure can communicate in different ways.

RECEIVING FEEDBACK ON STUDENT WORK

Students can use GenAI to receive feedback on their work. In order to do this, students copy and paste their work into a chatbot then ask for feedback. When teachers set up these chatbots, feedback can be tailored to the assignments. Teachers can add rubrics or source materials to the chatbots to focus responses further. Here are some ways to use GenAI for feedback:

- Provide general feedback on the work.

- Ask for ways to elaborate on underdeveloped areas.

- Ask to provide feedback on the clarity of the text.

- Have it check the text for redundancy.

- Tell GenAI to look for areas that can be revised or need further research.

- Check for spelling, grammar, and mechanical errors.

- Reformat the essay in MLA, APA, or Chicago style.

- Copy and paste the rubric and ask how the essay would score and what could be done to improve the writing.

With GenAI, students can get meaningful and personalized feedback that will empower them to become better writers, scientists, historians, or mathematicians. Not all students have the luxury of having someone in their home who can help them. However, GenAI makes it possible for all students to have a partner that can strengthen their work. GenAI helps level the playing field and provides more equitable opportunities for all students to be proficient writers across the content areas.

PROVIDING INTELLIGENT TUTORING AND RESEARCH ASSISTANCE

There is only so much time in the day. Teachers with 150 or more students cannot take the time to check in with every student every day and ensure that each student has a comprehensive understanding of critical learning, nor do they have the time to sit with every student and provide one-to-one tutoring. Not all students have access to learning support when they leave school. Not all students have access to someone at home who has a thorough understanding of essential topics or the Advanced Placement (AP) or International Baccalaureate (IB) coursework they may be looking to pursue. This is where GenAI can help. Chatbots can be used to help deepen student understanding of content or skills. With GenAI, every student can have access to a tutor, lab assistant, writing partner, or debate partner whenever and wherever they have Internet access. Consider the following:

Math: *A math tutor that helps students understand complex mathematical concepts and can offer guided practice*

Science: *A lab assistant that helps students collect and analyze data and assists with writing conclusions*

Language Arts: *A writing partner that can suggest starting points and transitions and give feedback to students to help revise and edit their final drafts*

Social Studies: *A debate opponent that can challenge students through Socratic questioning to help deepen their understanding of a topic and prepare them to defend their positions on this topic*

Chatbots are an excellent tool to support students who are conducting research. They can help stimulate student curiosity and support student research. Students can tell GenAI the topic they are researching and GenAI can assist with the research process. A GenAI companion can be more than just a search engine; it can be a personalized guide, cheerleader, and critical thinking buddy all rolled into one. Here's how:

Fueling curiosity: *Chatbots can engage students in active questioning, prompting them to think beyond keywords and explore new avenues.*

Demystifying the maze: *Information overload? No problem! Chatbots can sift through mountains of data, curate relevant sources, and even explain complex concepts in digestible chunks. This allows students to focus on understanding, rather than wrestle with overwhelming results.*

Building confidence: *Learning to research can be daunting, but chatbots provide a safe space to experiment and ask "silly" questions. The constant availability and nonjudgmental nature of working with a chatbot empowers students to explore freely and gain confidence in their ability to research.*

Tailoring to individual needs: *No two students learn the same way. Chatbots can personalize the research journey, adapting their responses to individual learning styles and preferences, ensuring every student gets the support they need.*

BRINGING CONTENT TO LIFE

With the plethora of digital content available to students outside of the classroom today, teachers can often feel as though they have to compete for their students' attention. Chatbots can be used in several ways to bring content to life. GenAI allows students to engage with content that is meaningful to them. Instead of watching a film that repeats the same narrative over and over, students can have conversations that are fresh and new each time they are launched. Students can ask questions that interest them and learn from experts who, in the past, have not been readily available to interact with them. With GenAI, teachers can program chatbots to act and respond as though they are historical figures or fictional characters in order to help solidify concepts being covered in class. Consider the following:

Math:

- AP Calculus students can learn from a significant mathematician, such as Albert Einstein, to understand the development of their work.

- Elementary students can learn how to multiply and divide fractions with a bot that responds in the voice of Shaggy from the cartoon *Scooby-Doo, Where Are You!*

Science:

- Chemistry students can have a conversation with Madame Curie about her work with radium or her work to help cure cancer.

- Earth science students can discuss the workings of a volcano or the makeup of cells with Bill Nye.

Language Arts:

- Middle school students studying *The Diary of Anne Frank* can learn more about her experience in hiding during the Nazi persecution of the Jewish people.

- Elementary students can discuss the writing process with Dave Pilkey to learn from his experience as a writer.

Social Studies:

- U.S. history students can have a conversation with Dr. Martin Luther King, Jr., about his work with the civil rights movement.

- Students of ancient civilizations can discuss the importance of establishing laws and civil codes with the Mesopotamian King Hammurabi.

A LOOK AT CLASSROOM RESEARCH

When ChatGPT became widely available, Jason wanted to test it in his classroom. He wanted to investigate the question, "How can GenAI improve student writing?" To answer this question, he decided to conduct an action research project with his freshman English classes.

The goal of the experiment was to track and compare student writing growth across three explanatory writing prompts (see Table 3.1). Three sections of freshman English were involved in this research, and the classes were labeled as follows:

- **Class C:** Control group. No extra interventions.

- **Class T:** Mentor Text. This class reviewed ChatGPT-generated responses, scored them using the rubric, and discussed the strengths and weaknesses of ChatGPT's responses before responding to the prompts themselves.

- **Class G:** ChatGPT. Students outlined an essay, and then the outline was given to ChatGPT. Students were provided a printed copy of the ChatGPT response based on their outline. Students used the printed copies as a guide while they responded to the prompt. Though students had paper copies of how ChatGPT would write their essays, they were instructed to do their own writing. Students borrowed phrasing and words from the ChatGPT examples but largely did their own writing.

TABLE 3.1 AVERAGE SCORES AND OVERALL GROWTH FROM CLASSROOM RESEARCH

GROUP NAME	PROMPT 1 AVERAGE SCORE (OUT OF 20)	PROMPT 3 AVERAGE SCORE (OUT OF 20)	AVERAGE STUDENT GROWTH FROM PROMPT 1 TO PROMPT 3
Class C (Control)	13	15.15	10.75%
Class T (Mentor Text)	14	15.62	8.10%
Class G (ChatGPT)	13.68	17.87	20.95%
Students with IEPs in Class G	11.2	16.6	27.00%

The class that used ChatGPT the most, Class G, exhibited a 20.95% growth rate from prompt 1 to prompt 3. Student writing scores for Class G improved approximately twice as much as writing scores in the other two classes. Allowing students to use ChatGPT intentionally doubled the improvement in student writing.

Class G also had five students supported by IEPs. This is a tiny sample size, but the results are impressive. These students' scores improved by 27% on average. They started with lower average scores on prompt 1 compared to all of the classes. However, by prompt 3, their average scores exceeded the average scores of students in Class T and Class C. These students demonstrated the most gain, suggesting that students with special needs may have the most to gain from using GenAI. This mirrors research discussed by Ethan Mollick (2023) where he says that GenAI often helps those with the lowest skills the most.

Students supported by IEPs often can verbally articulate clear ideas and even come up with some evidence or reasoning to support their position. However, some students may struggle with organization and focus in their writing. Having ChatGPT create sample writing based on their ideas was highly effective. It gave students a template to follow that was based on their thinking. Used in this way, GenAI helped students communicate their thinking more effectively, rather than just doing the thinking for them.

As a result of the class research, the largest benefit to student writing appeared to be that students were more organized and could articulate their ideas more clearly while using GenAI. Table 3.2 provides some practical recommendations that we learned from conducting the classroom action research.

TABLE 3.2   TIPS FOR USING GenAI TO SUPPORT ESSAY WRITING

HOW TO SUPPORT SMALL GROUPS OF STUDENTS	HOW TO USE CHATGPT TO SUPPORT WHOLE CLASSES
• Have students write an outline of their response to the prompt. • The teacher (or aide) feeds the prompt and the outline to GenAI and tells it to write an essay that responds to the prompt and includes the ideas in the outline. • Students are given copies of GenAI responses based on their outlines. • Students respond to the prompt using the generated AI responses as a guide.	• Have students write an outline of their response to the prompt. • Students feed the prompt and outline to GenAI and tell GenAI to write an essay that responds to the prompt and includes the ideas in the outline. • Students respond to the prompt using the generated AI responses as a guide. • After writing the essay, the students complete a reflection and explain the difference between their essay and the one produced by GenAI. • Another option is to have students annotate their work and explain the differences.

The Big Ideas

Chapter 3 shared how GenAI can be used to improve learning experiences for students:

- **GenAI personalizes learning:** GenAI can adjust learning materials and pace based on a student's strengths and weaknesses. It can also provide feedback and answer student's questions in real time.

- **GenAI improves engagement:** GenAI can make learning more engaging by providing automated feedback, creating content customized to student preferences, and translating languages.

- **GenAI supports students with disabilities:** GenAI tools like text-to-speech and closed captioning can help students with disabilities access learning materials.

- **GenAI helps students write:** GenAI can help students brainstorm ideas and overcome writer's block by generating drafts based on student prompts. Students can revise and edit these drafts to improve their writing.

- **GenAI provides feedback:** GenAI can analyze student work and provide feedback on grammar, clarity, and areas that need improvement.

- **GenAI acts as a tutor:** GenAI chatbots can act like tutors, lab assistants, writing partners, or debate partners. They can answer questions, explain concepts, and help students practice skills.

- **GenAI brings content to life:** GenAI chatbots can be programmed to act like historical figures or fictional characters to help students learn about different topics.

- **GenAI assists with research:** GenAI chatbots can help students with research by finding relevant sources, explaining complex concepts, and answering questions.

Overall, GenAI can be a valuable tool to support student learning and make education more engaging and accessible.

You Try It: Student Prompt Engineering

Help students engineer effective prompts to improve their writing.

What You'll Need:

- Student access to GenAI such as ChatGPT or Gemini.

- An essay prompt or guidelines for students to use while crafting their essays.

(Continued)

(Continued)

Instructions:

1. Prompt engineering: Tell students to engineer a prompt to write an essay that includes their research and any additional information they feel is important to the writing.

2. Generate multiple drafts: Have students generate three versions of the response and highlight words, phrases, and sentences that are unique to each draft.

3. Identify and explain: Ask students to explain how these nuances change the tone or voice of the writing.

4. Select best examples: After they have completed this, have them underline the words, sentences, and phrases that they prefer in each draft.

5. Reflect: Challenge students to explain what they liked and then have them construct a new essay using what they underlined.

Questions for Reflection

1. How might GenAI be used at different stages of a challenging task to support students who struggle with important concepts?

2. When students use GenAI to generate drafts or receive feedback, how can you ensure students are still actively engaged in the writing process and that their work reflects their own voice and ideas?

3. How can you use GenAI to encourage students to become critical thinkers when GenAI can generate information for them so quickly?

4. How might GenAI spark curiosity and encourage students to become lifelong learners?

www.beyondthe curriculum.net/ book-1/chapter-3

Follow the link or scan the QR code for more helpful resources related to the content found in Chapter 3.

ETHICS IN THE AGE OF AI

A Message From Jason

Years ago, our school had a minor scandal. A popular athlete, on the verge of graduation, admitted in a public presentation that he had never written any of his essays nor read any of the novels he was supposed to have read. The presentation was a final graduation requirement, and some of the assessors wanted to fail the student as a result. However, administrators decided his presentation met the standard and he was allowed to pass. School staff were upset and offended but, in the end, the student graduated.

This unfortunate example underscores the need to teach ethical behavior. We'll never be able to stop all cheating, but we need to create clear expectations with our students to help them understand ethical behavior. These expectations also communicate the importance of students doing their own work and their own thinking.

It's very easy to get caught up in the negative aspects of cheating. I find myself still reflexively trying to catch students cheating when I think their work doesn't sound quite right. However, this mindset misses the larger points when considering student learning and ethical behavior.

GenAI further muddies the waters when it comes to ethics and cheating. As an educator, I was frustrated that the student got away with cheating in such a brazen manner. Part of my frustration stemmed from the fact that there was a misalignment between the skills I wanted the student to learn and the way I went about assessing those skills. I was making learning only about what I wanted, rather than what students wanted or needed.

(Continued)

(Continued)

One of the big shifts I have made in my own teaching since then is to emphasize student thinking and look for opportunities to create two-way dialogues with each student about the work they are doing. Instead of asking comprehension questions about something they read, I might take a class period to interview each student individually about the reading. These conversations can include areas where the student may have struggled with the reading so that I can correct misunderstandings or practice different strategies to understand the text. Talking about students with the work they are doing while they are doing it gives them timely feedback and help as they need it. Students are far less likely to take shortcuts or try to cheat when you are giving them help and feedback as the work is occurring instead of after the work has occurred.

What is the definition of authentic student learning? GenAI challenges educators to think about what ethics means. Who is the arbiter of ethics? Remember that teachers make up stuff all the time, including what "ethical behavior" is. Working with a friend may be considered "cheating" in one classroom, while in another it is lauded as effective collaboration. Even in my own classroom, these expectations can shift from assignment to assignment. Ethical behavior should reflect not only what the teacher wants, but also what the students need. In many cases, students don't want to cheat but may feel they have no other choice left. An effective code of ethics will consider the skills students need to engage in the world outside of school, including how to use GenAI to learn from mistakes and fix those mistakes when they occur. There is not one right code of ethics out there.

An effective code of ethics will unlock the unlimited potential inside our classroom by fostering positive behaviors and allowing students to learn in ways that work for them. Remember, students live up to our expectations of them, whether those expectations are positive or negative. Let's reframe our thinking on ethics as opportunities that challenge our students to grow.

Jason

The purpose of education is to shape students' skills, talents, and attitudes so that they can critically engage in the world today and in the future. It is important to be deliberate in this process, which is why educators need to be thoughtful about how they use GenAI. Students are discovering GenAI with or without their teachers, so it is our challenge as educators to guide students toward its ethical use.

One of the first considerations in integrating GenAI ethically is to ensure it is being used in age-appropriate ways. Not all students are ready to use GenAI. Educators must consider why they are teaching GenAI, decide what resources to provide their students, and preemptively address concerns that arise from GenAI use. Table 4.1 provides some guidance for age-appropriate use of GenAI.

TABLE 4.1   AGE-APPROPRIATE USES OF GenAI

GRADE LEVEL	WHY TEACH GenAI	RESOURCES	CONSIDERATIONS
K–Second	• Many have previously been exposed to GenAI • Sparks curiosity • Promotes digital literacy • Develops critical thinking • Builds a foundation for future learning	• Google • Quick, Draw! • Canva (Image generation) • MagicStudent • AI for Kids	• Young children tend to think GenAI is a real person. • Although GenAI can be a learning tool, hands-on experiences are still crucial.
Third–Fifth	• Enhances learning materials • Models • Builds critical thinking skills • Promotes digital literacy • Fosters creativity • Prepares for the future	• Demonstrate the use of ChatGPT and/or Gemini • Canva (Image generation) • MagicStudent • Code.org • AI for Kids	• AI shouldn't replace trial and error. • Help students understand potential risks and appropriate use of GenAI. • Use care when selecting tools.
Middle School	• Fosters critical thinking of GenAI outputs • Empowers responsible use • Develops digital literacy • Fosters curiosity and innovation • Enhances learning	**Teaching Fact Checking:** • NewsGuard • Snopes • FactCheck.org • Google Odd One Out **General Resources:** • MagicStudent • Code.org • AI for Kids • Canva (Image generation)	• Unrestricted access to GenAI could expose students to inappropriate content. • Students can make risky decisions when interacting with GenAI. • AI outputs can contain errors or biases.

(Continued)

GRADE LEVEL	WHY TEACH GenAI	RESOURCES	CONSIDERATIONS
High School	• Develops critical thinking about GenAI • Helps understand GenAI limitations • Boosts digital literacy • Prepares for the future • Develops GenAI responsibly • Builds on existing skills	**Teaching Fact Checking:** • NewsGuard • Snopes • FactCheck.org • Google Odd One Out **General Resources:** • MagicStudent • Teachable Machine • Partnership on GenAI • Canva (Image generation)	• Emphasize critical thinking and verification of information from GenAI sources. • Highlight potential risks and teach students about responsible GenAI use. • Be mindful of not overwhelming students with resources.

Adapted from Prothero (2024).

ETHICS AND GenAI

English novelist George Elliot once wrote, "Our deeds determine us as much as we determine our deeds." Our actions define who we are. This is why it is so important to use GenAI in honest, ethical ways. If GenAI is used to cheat or avoid thinking, then a user becomes a person who cheats and avoids thinking in life. One of the best ways to help ensure we are using GenAI properly is to create a code of ethics.

GenAI CODE OF ETHICS

When using GenAI, I will…

1. use it to brainstorm and support my learning.

2. only provide data or work to GenAI that does not contain any student information or identifiers.

3. **always check the output** before using it with students, parents, or colleagues.

4. be honest and upfront with students about what material was produced using GenAI, especially questions, activities, writing, and examples.

5. only use quotes, data, or information provided by GenAI if I can verify it independently.

A code of ethics can be both a guide and a reminder. It dictates how teachers interact with GenAI and serves as a great reminder when important deadlines loom. Jason has written his personal code of ethics and posted it where he can see it every day in his classroom.

This code of ethics isn't long (shorter codes are often more effective), but it provides a daily reminder of how to use this technology appropriately. One special note about point number four: Modeling how and when we use GenAI in front of students is important so that students see how to use it ethically. If educators try to hide their use of GenAI, in a kind of "man behind the curtain, Wizard of Oz" style, students will hide their use of GenAI as well.

Publishing a code of ethics and being upfront with students helps maintain the appropriate use of GenAI. It is a powerful tool that improves education. However, the use of a code of ethics should not just be limited to teachers. Students should also use a code of ethics when interacting with GenAI.

Before creating a code of ethics, here are some things to consider:

Involve students in writing the code of ethics. Student investment is important to generate buy-in. Students will be more likely to follow a code of ethics they have helped develop, as they are owners of this code.

Demonstrate different ways that GenAI can be used. Before writing a code of ethics, students need to be well-versed in GenAI. Spend time introducing GenAI to the classroom and demonstrate the different ways it can be used. This is true even in schools that have policies in place restricting the use of GenAI because some students will still be using these tools on devices outside of school.

Engage students in effective and responsible practice of GenAI tools. If students don't know or do not have practice, they will use GenAI to craft superficial answers, and they won't even be aware of how shallow those answers are. Following a code of ethics means students are less likely to get the GenAI to do their thinking for them and more likely to engage in meaningful collaboration with GenAI. This, in turn, will help build the collaborative critical thinking skills necessary for future success.

Demonstrate the ways GenAI fails or does a poor job. Students will be better served knowing both the strengths and weaknesses of the technology. Give students an assignment that requires them to critique the output of GenAI. They can then share those critiques in small groups or whole-class discussions.

LESSON: WRITING A CLASS CODE OF ETHICS

Once students have had time to engage with GenAI themselves and know more about what to expect when using GenAI, it is time to start writing a class code of ethics.

Here is a lesson outline for an introduction to GenAI:

Day 1: Explain what GenAI is, give access/sign up for GenAI, and play around with fun prompts. Have students share their favorite prompts.

Day 2: Use GenAI to help write and revise an in-class writing prompt.

Day 3: Ask GenAI to read, summarize, and write questions about a text. Students should critique the summary and questions.

Day 4: Have students ask GenAI to write directions for a task the student knows how to do. Students then critique those directions.

Day 5: Have students compare GenAI answers with Google search results. Students should reflect and explain which results they found more trustworthy.

TEACHER REFLECTIONS

- What patterns did you notice about how GenAI was used by students?

- After seeing students use it, what questions do you still have about GenAI in your classroom?

- Share questions with students and have another discussion about it.

STEPS FOR WRITING A CLASS CODE OF ETHICS

Step 1: Consider the Nonnegotiables

This code of ethics is one that both teachers and students will abide by. If there are uses of GenAI that the teacher is not comfortable with, they should tell students at the beginning of the process. One of the benefits of having students contribute to the code is to give them agency in the classroom. When students come up with a code of ethics and it is immediately vetoed it deprives students of agency, so it is important for teachers to share their nonnegotiables in order to avoid having to veto student input.

There may also be other restrictions placed upon students by the school or the platforms themselves, such as user age restrictions or district policies. It is OK to acknowledge that some of these policies may have room for improvement, but students and staff still need to follow them. Be sure that students are aware of these factors before starting the code of ethics. Remind students that ultimately, following a code of ethics ensures ethical behavior.

Step 2: Brainstorm and Categorize

After nonnegotiables are established, have students brainstorm a list of ways they might use GenAI. The goal is to have students categorize which uses of GenAI are appropriate and which ones are not. The bigger the list, the better. One effective strategy is to give each student a stack of sticky notes to write their ideas on. Be sure to have students only write one idea per sticky note! These sticky notes are then posted on a whiteboard for everyone to see. The class (or the teacher) can manipulate sticky notes to place similar ideas into categories. For teachers who prefer to work digitally or even remotely, a digital whiteboard has similar functionalities. The ideas in Figure 4.1 have already been categorized.

FIGURE 4.1   SAMPLE CLASS BRAINSTORMING AND CATEGORIZING

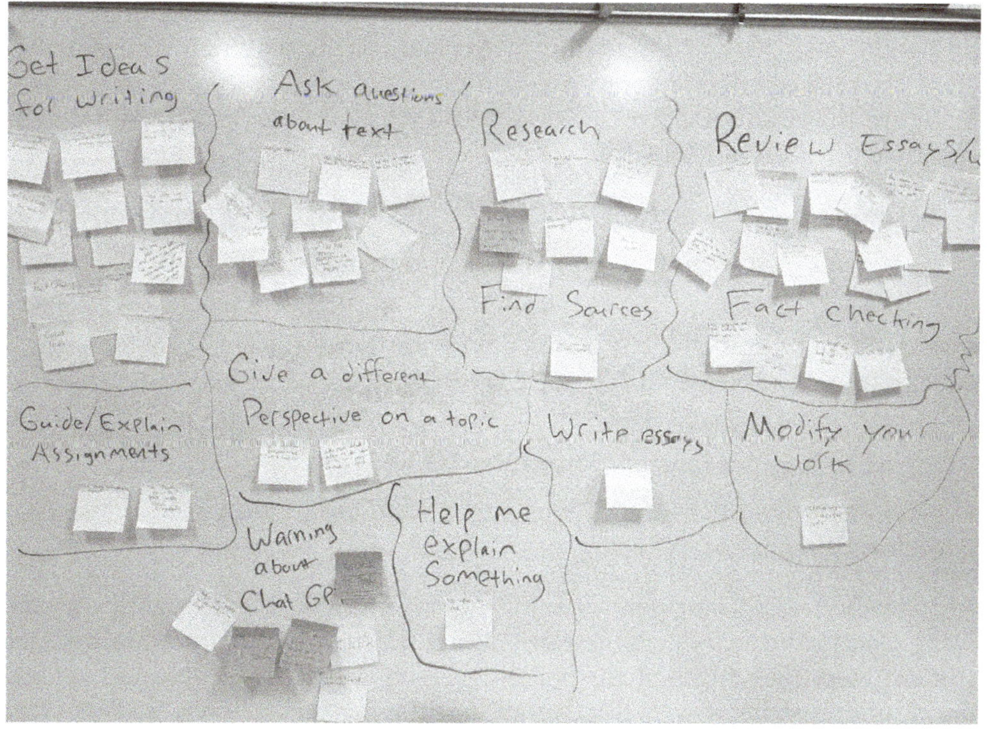

Step 3: Discuss

Allow students time, either in small groups or as a whole class, to discuss the ideas/categories generated. Make sure to push students to talk about the positives and negatives of each idea/category. If students are unsure whether it is appropriate to use GenAI for something, have them replace GenAI with the name of their friend. Is it OK to ask Billy for ideas on how to start my essay? Is it OK to ask Fernanda to write my essay? This may help students clarify use cases for GenAI.

Step 4: Vote

After ideas have been combined and discussed, it is time to vote on which uses of GenAI are appropriate and allowable. These votes will become the basis of the class code of ethics.

A simple Google Form can be used to vote. Generally, using a 1–4 Likert Scale, where 1 means strongly disagree and 4 means strongly agree, will give the best idea of where students are. It is important to not have a middle number where students can be neutral. Tell students they have to take a stand on each issue.

After voting is concluded, compile the results. If results are overwhelmingly one-sided, it is easy to put that rule into a code of ethics. If the results are mixed, further discussions with the class are warranted, especially if the results are in the 45 percent– to 65 percent–approval range. This range of results indicates students may be confused about how to use GenAI. When this is the case, further discussion or explanation is required. Additionally, ideas may be subdivided into smaller parts to generate more agreement. Here are the results from a senior English class, in which 25 seniors were surveyed after using ChatGPT.

- 96 percent of students felt it was appropriate to use GenAI to generate ideas

- 76 percent of students felt it was appropriate to use GenAI to help start writing

- 80 percent of students felt it was appropriate to use GenAI to generate sample essays to look at

- 56 percent of students felt it was appropriate to use GenAI as a search engine to look up information

- 84 percent of students felt it was appropriate to use GenAI to revise their writing

Most responses tilt strongly one way or another. However, feelings about using GenAI as a search engine were mixed. The teacher analyzed individual student responses and had further discussions with students to understand the responses better. It was discovered that the less tech-savvy a student was, the more likely they were to embrace using GenAI as a search engine. More tech-savvy students (those who better understood how to prompt engineer) were vehemently opposed to using GenAI as a search engine. This suggested that the main issue was understanding the limitations of GenAI. More work as a class was needed on why or why not to use GenAI as a search engine.

One final observation the teacher had when examining the data was that students who were more traditional rule followers were less likely to embrace GenAI. This was true even for students who struggled with writing and English Language Arts in general. These are students who, according to the research in Chapter 3, stood to benefit the most from using it. Public perception of GenAI is shifting, but currently, many people view GenAI as something that makes it too easy to cheat. In fact, a Pew survey of teachers in 2024 found that 25 percent thought ChatGPT did more harm than good, while only 6 percent said it benefited more than harmed (Lin, 2024). GenAI may still have a negative reputation, and this may be why those students shied away from embracing it.

Step 5: Revise

After the code of ethics has been compiled, have the class check the result. Make sure students sign off on the finished product and that it accurately reflects their understanding of how and when to use GenAI. If it doesn't, keep revising! More discussion and voting may be necessary.

Step 6: Publish

Make sure students can easily refer to their code of ethics after it is adopted. It should be displayed in the classroom and communicated to student families as well. See Table 4.2 for a sample student code of ethics.

Having a clear code of ethics will help students and teachers if concerns about use arise in the future. Additionally, by having students take the lead in writing this code of ethics, they will be more engaged and more likely to follow it.

TABLE 4.2   SAMPLE STUDENT CODE OF ETHICS

1. It is OK to use GenAI to brainstorm and get ideas for writing.

2. GenAI can be used to get a different perspective on a topic.

3. GenAI can be used to summarize and ask questions about articles and shorter text.

4. Because we can't trust and confirm information from GenAI, it should not be used for research, fact-checking, or finding sources.

5. GenAI can help explain assignments and ask questions to get help when I don't understand something.

6. GenAI should be used to revise and edit essays and other work.

7. Beyond basic editing and revisions, GenAI should not be used to create or modify work unless the assignment specifically asks you to do so.

TEACHING STUDENTS HOW TO USE GenAI EFFECTIVELY

In the movie *The Empire Strikes Back,* while attempting to escape the Empire, Han Solo navigates the Millennium Falcon into an asteroid field. As he approaches it, C3PO, an android companion, interjects, "Sir, the possibility of successfully navigating an asteroid field is approximately 3,720 to 1." Han Solo replies, "Never tell me the odds" (Lucas, 1980).

This scene highlights the role of GenAI and the responsibility of the end user. C3PO provides Solo with data. The data is irrefutable and, more than likely, accurate. However, it is completely up to Solo to use the information and make a decision that will best serve him, his crew, and passengers. Ultimately, Han Solo ignored the data provided by C3PO. Flying into the asteroid field helped save the lives of Solo and his friends, which eventually led to the overthrow of the evil Empire. Had Han Solo relied exclusively on the information from C3PO, rather than using his own judgment, who knows what would have happened.

AI helps to streamline the work we do. It can generate reports, write emails, construct slide decks for presentations, produce images, and more. It simplifies tasks, but it does not alleviate the responsibility of the end user. Rather, it challenges the end user to review the product to ensure its quality. This is an essential skill that will help students become twenty-first-century critical thinkers. Teachers should emphasize this skill to help prepare students to engage in the world beyond the classroom.

It is all too easy to rely on GenAI to do the work. And because GenAI is not accountable to anyone, it is the end user who is responsible when they publish and share the work GenAI creates for them. There are consequences for a lack of ethical use of GenAI. For example, a New York lawyer had ChatGPT write a brief that was presented to a judge. While reading it, the judge reviewed the cited cases and could not find them. It was determined that these cases were completely made up. Because of this, the lawyer was fined (Bohannon, 2023).

As of September 2024, the ChatGPT website warns users that "When you use our Services you understand and agree: Output may not always be accurate. You should not rely on Output from our Services as a sole source of truth or factual information, or as a substitute for professional advice" (OpenAI, 2023). Because GenAI can produce misinformation, educators need to teach students how to use it effectively and ethically.

THE IMPORTANCE OF LATERAL READING

In the age of AI, students need to learn to be critical thinkers. Although GenAI holds immense potential to personalize and enhance learning, we must focus on ensuring the accuracy of AI-generated content. Here's where a critical thinking strategy called "lateral reading" comes in.

Traditional reading involves a linear progression from sentence to sentence within a single source. Think about reading a book. Readers start at the beginning and read line to line, page to page until they reach the end of the book. Lateral reading, however, breaks free from this linear path. It encourages students to explore information "laterally," venturing beyond the initial source to verify its claims and assess its credibility. Lateral reading also helps students gain a deeper understanding of a subject and further builds background knowledge of a subject.

Imagine students with multiple browser tabs open after reading an article—they're investigating the author's background, the website's reputation, and fact-checking claims from the article against established sources. This multisource exploration empowers them with the tools to discern fact from fallacy.

The age of AI presents students with an uncharted sea of information, much of it from questionable sources. Lateral reading cultivates "source literacy" in students. They learn to evaluate the reliability of GenAI outputs to ensure the validity of the information presented. It empowers students to distinguish reliable outputs from GenAI hallucinations—when GenAI generates inaccurate or nonsensical information in response to a user prompt. Furthermore, by exposing students to various perspectives on the same topic through different sources, students become aware of potential biases inherent in GenAI models trained on vast datasets. Lateral reading fosters a critical analysis of information, enabling students to form well-rounded conclusions.

Generative AI can produce texts that, on the surface, appear to be convincingly authoritative. Many students will take outputs verbatim and trust that GenAI is providing them with reliable information. Lateral reading equips students to go beyond the surface fluency. By teaching students to verify statistics, research authors, and compare information with established sources, students can identify AI-generated content that lacks factual grounding.

Lateral reading goes beyond simply fact-checking AI-generated content. It fosters a deeper research approach. Students actively seek evidence from various sources, compare information, and synthesize findings. This not only equips them to navigate the complexities of AI-generated content but also strengthens their overall research skills—a valuable asset not just in the classroom, but throughout their academic and personal lives.

In a world saturated with information, lateral reading promotes independent thinking. GenAI can provide information efficiently and effectively. However, GenAI can generate information that is inaccurate, laden with bias, and lacks clarity with respect to the needs of the user.

Lateral reading helps students learn to question what they read, to verify information, and to form their own informed opinions. This empowers them to be critical consumers of information, not simply passive recipients. The following pages will discuss some of the major concerns with GenAI and will offer lesson ideas to help students master lateral reading, allowing them to develop the critical thinking skills they need to thrive in the age of AI. It will help students to become lifelong learners who can separate fact from fiction in any information landscape.

THE ABCS OF ETHICAL AI USE

To help students learn how to use GenAI, it is important to help them view the product of GenAI through critical lenses. When doing so, we want students to ask themselves the following questions:

- Is it Accurate?

- Is it Biased?

- Is it Clear to my point?

As described in Chapter 1, chatbots are GenAI that use Large Language Models to mimic human speech. It attempts to sound authoritative and can be convincing. Allowing GenAI to take away human agency does not alleviate our responsibility. Users are accountable for the content GenAI produces. The ABCs of GenAI are three simple steps that students can easily master to promote more ethical use of GenAI.

Accuracy

The first question students must ask as they review GenAI outputs is, "Is this accurate?" GenAI is known to make up information and relate it in compelling ways. Checking sources is crucial yet simple to accomplish. Teaching students to keyword-search phrases from the output and cross-check it helps them to evaluate the accuracy of what GenAI produces. This is an important skill to teach students as many will want to simply have GenAI produce something for them and accept it as accurate.

LESSON: CHECKING GenAI OUTPUT FOR ACCURACY

Here is a lateral reading activity you can try with your students that will teach them how to check an GenAI output for accuracy:

1. Explain to students that GenAI is a type of technology that can be used to create text, images, and other forms of media. GenAI can be used to generate realistic and convincing content, but it is important to remember that AI-generated content can also be inaccurate.

2. Show students how to search for information on a particular topic and how to evaluate the credibility of the source.

3. Tell students that they will be playing a game called "Two Truths and One Lie." In this game, students will read an article that provides three facts about volcanoes, and they will have to identify which fact is a lie.

4. Read the sample article on volcanoes, below.

5. Challenge students to collaborate to uncover the lie. They can discuss what they know about volcanoes and use the Internet to fact-check information.

6. Have students share their answers with the class.

7. Reveal the lie to students.

8. Discuss the importance of checking the accuracy of information before using it. Explain that inaccurate information can lead to bad decisions and can be harmful.

Facts About Volcanoes (an Essay Written by ChatGPT)

Volcanoes have fascinated humanity for millennia, their explosive eruptions and molten fury captivating our imagination. The very word "volcano" evokes images of fiery mountains spewing lava and ash into the sky. But how do these geological wonders erupt? In this essay, we will delve into the intricate process behind volcanic eruptions, shedding light on this interesting phenomenon.

At the heart of every volcano lies a magma chamber, a reservoir filled with molten rock and gas. The magma chamber is akin to a pressurized time bomb, as it is the primary source of volcanic eruptions. As magma rises from the Earth's mantle, it accumulates in this chamber. Over time, the pressure builds up, much like shaking a carbonated beverage. When the pressure becomes too great, the volcano erupts, releasing its pent-up energy in the form of lava, ash, and gas.

Volcanoes are predictable. While scientific advances have certainly improved our ability to monitor volcanic activity, predicting the exact timing and intensity of an eruption remains a significant challenge. Volcanic behavior depends on a complex interplay of factors, including the composition of the magma, gas content, and the volcano's historical patterns. Seismologists and volcanologists use various tools, such as seismometers and gas monitoring stations, to detect warning signs. However, predicting precisely when a volcano will erupt with pinpoint accuracy remains elusive, making them unpredictable and potentially dangerous natural phenomena.

Volcanoes are not a one-size-fits-all phenomenon. There are various types of volcanic eruptions, each characterized by distinct characteristics and outcomes. The two most common types are explosive eruptions and effusive eruptions. Explosive eruptions, like the infamous Mount St. Helens eruption in 1980, are characterized by violent explosions that send massive amounts of ash and debris into the atmosphere. In contrast, effusive eruptions, exemplified by Hawaii's Kilauea volcano, involve the steady flow of lava, which oozes out relatively calmly, allowing nearby residents and scientists to monitor and study the eruption more safely.

In conclusion, the world of volcanic eruptions is a complex and captivating one. From the underlying magma chambers and diverse eruption types to the compelling challenges of prediction, volcanoes continue to inspire awe and curiosity. While we have uncovered two intriguing facts about these fiery giants, it's crucial to remember that predicting their behavior remains a daunting task, leaving us to marvel at their unpredictable yet mesmerizing displays of Earth's raw power.

Correct Answer: The sentence stating "Volcanoes are predictable" is the lie in this article.

To determine the lie in the exercise above, students either had to have strong background knowledge about volcanoes or engage in lateral reading. In this case, students would read other websites about volcanoes, find discrepancies between the original text and new websites, and then determine which fact in the original was a lie.

Lateral reading also has the benefit of building context and background knowledge. The more students read about a topic, the more they understand the topic and the more likely they are to question information that may be false, especially plausible-sounding info from GenAI.

Bias

Large Language Models, such as ChatGPT and Gemini, are trained on information that is publicly shared on the Internet (OpenAI, n.d.). Because chatbots lack morals or understanding, they use the data set that best responds to a prompt using information from the Internet that demonstrates high levels of reliability. Since the Internet is mostly produced by white males in the United States, the chatbot most often takes on that voice (Jesutofunmi et al., 2023). It then relays information from that data source without analyzing the output to ensure that it is sensitive to various groups of people. Thus, it is the responsibility of the end user to be critical of the outputs produced by GenAI before publishing them.

When prompted to write a vocabulary list for a unit on westward expansion for sixth-grade students, ChatGPT provided a list that included the following results:

Frontier: The unexplored or undeveloped region at the edge of a settled area.

Pioneer: A person who is one of the first to explore or settle a new country or area.

Homestead: A piece of land that someone can acquire and live on, often given by the government to encourage settlement of an area.

There is nothing inherently biased with the list of words above. These are words our sixth-grade students probably should know as they are exploring a unit on westward expansion. However, the definitions of these words can be harmful and perpetuate a Eurocentric, white-supremacist understanding of the world.

The regions west of the Mississippi that white settlers were seeking had already been explored and developed by many indigenous peoples. These lands contained many thriving communities that had lived there for thousands of years before wagon trains arrived. Finally, the lands that were "given by the government" were taken from other people. To share ChatGPT's definitions with sixth-grade students would be irresponsible and insensitive. Teachers need to be critical of what GenAI produces and teach students how to analyze GenAI outputs for biases such as these.

LESSON: EVALUATING GenAI OUTPUT FOR BIAS

Try this lesson with your students to help them learn how to use lateral reading and evaluate AI-generated outputs with a critical lens:

1. Begin by defining bias. Explain that bias is a prejudice in favor of or against one thing, person, or group compared with another, usually in a way that is considered to be unfair.

2. Discuss different types of bias:

   Emotional bias: This type of bias is based on our emotions, such as our likes and dislikes. For example, if we have a strong negative opinion about a particular group of people, we may be more likely to believe negative things about them.

   Confirmation bias: This type of bias is the tendency to seek out information that confirms our existing beliefs and to ignore information that contradicts them. For example, if we believe that climate change is a hoax, we may be more likely to read articles that support that belief and ignore articles that contradict it.

   Stereotyping: This type of bias is the tendency to make assumptions about people based on their group membership. For example, we may assume that all members of a particular group are lazy or dishonest, even though there is no evidence to support this.

   Attribution bias: This type of bias is the tendency to attribute our successes to our abilities and our failures to external factors. For example, if we get a good grade on a test, we may attribute it to our intelligence, but if we get a bad grade, we may attribute it to the difficulty of the test or the unfairness of the teacher.

3. Once students have a basic understanding of bias, give them the list of vocabulary words on westward expansion (or any other topic with biased vocabulary words) and ask them to identify what kinds of biases are present in the definitions.

   Frontier: The unexplored or undeveloped region at the edge of a settled area.

   Pioneer: A person who is one of the first to explore or settle a new country or area.

   Homestead: A piece of land that someone can acquire and live on, often given by the government to encourage settlement of an area.

4. As students identify bias, help them to explain how it is affecting the way they interpret the information. Ask them who might benefit from these definitions and who may be harmed.

5. After students have examined bias in this list, have them rewrite the definitions in ways that eliminate the bias.

6. Discuss the importance of being aware of bias. Explain that bias can affect the way we interpret information, and that it is important to be able to identify it so that we can make informed decisions.

When students use GenAI to generate material, challenge them to check for bias in the response. Tell them to ask GenAI to identify any biases that may be included in the generated output. Students can further partner with GenAI to become conscientious and responsible citizens who are aware of the impact their work may have.

Students can also use lateral reading to check for biases within the content they consume. Encourage students to open a news article or other Internet source in one tab and a chatbot in another tab. Have students copy and paste the content into the chatbot and ask it to identify what kinds of biases might be found within the source.

Helping students identify the bias can empower them to be responsible consumers of information, develop empathy, and allow them to promote more inclusive spaces.

AI generates products quickly and efficiently. Most of the time, it produces content that satisfies the expectations of the end user. However, GenAI cannot get inside the user's mind. It does not know exactly what the user wants to create. It simply makes programmed guesses, like predictive text. It makes some good suggestions, but it ultimately only knows what the user includes in the prompt.

How to prompt engineer is an essential skill students need to learn to ensure that GenAI generates the product they intended. However, even the best prompts can miss the intended mark. Effective prompt engineering can help with things like intended audience, voice, and purpose.

The image below was generated by GenAI. The intent was to create an image for an upcoming football game between two high schools. One school's mascot is the eagle and the other school's is the trapper. When GenAI was prompted to create an image with an eagle and Davy Crockett fighting one another, it came up with the image of this anthropomorphic eagle. It did not hit the intended mark. This is a clear example of how GenAI lacked an understanding of our intentions.

Created by Aaron Blackwelder via Canva.com

LESSON: CONSIDERING CLARITY WITH GenAI OUTPUT

Here is a lateral reading activity you can do with your students:

1. Have students choose a sonnet by William Shakespeare. Copy and paste the poem into a chatbot and have it rewrite it with more modern language. Have them compare the two pieces of writing to see the differences in the poems. (See the example below).

2. Ask students the following questions:

   - What are some lines or phrases in the original text that are difficult for you to understand?

   - What are some lines or phrases generated by GenAI that make the poem easier to read?

   - What are some lines or phrases in the original poem that are vivid and poetic?

   - What are some lines or phrases generated by GenAI that lack emotion or vividness?

   - Does the AI-generated version help provide a better understanding of the poem to a novice reader of Shakespeare?

   - Why might it be helpful to provide AI-generated text to novice readers of Shakespeare?

   - What do you feel is lost in only reading the AI-generated version? What emotions are lost? What artistry is forgone?

3. Discuss the appeal of both pieces of writing.

Sonnet 18	Modern AI-Generated Rendition
Shall I compare thee to a summer's day?	Shall I compare you to a perfect summer day?
Thou art more lovely and more temperate.	You're even more beautiful and moderate.
Rough winds do shake the darling buds of May,	Harsh winds can disturb the precious May blossoms,
And summer's lease hath all too short a date.	And summer's time is far too fleeting.
Sometime too hot the eye of heaven shines,	Sometimes, the sun's intensity becomes overwhelming,
And often is his gold complexion dimmed;	And frequently, its golden complexion is obscured.
And every fair from fair sometime declines,	Every beautiful thing eventually loses its charm,

By chance, or nature's changing course, untrimmed;

Due to chance or the natural course of change, untrimmed.

But thy eternal summer shall not fade,

But your beauty will never wither away,

Nor lose possession of that fair thou ow'st,

Nor will you ever lose the beauty you possess.

Nor shall death brag thou wand'rest in his shade,

Death won't be able to claim you as its own,

When in eternal lines to Time thou grow'st.

When you continue to exist in timeless verses.

So long as men can breathe, or eyes can see,

As long as people can breathe and see with their eyes,

So long lives this, and this gives life to thee.

This poem will endure, and it will keep you alive.

In the example featured in the previous lesson, the teacher created a second reading for students with GenAI. By focusing on clarity, different versions of the same text are created to enable all students to understand a version of the text that meets their needs. By comparing multiple versions side by side, students can evaluate the strengths and weaknesses of GenAI-produced text.

Because GenAI is rapidly embedding itself into many corners of our lives, educators are challenged to help students navigate its ethical use. GenAI offers possibilities to enhance student learning. However, with great power comes great responsibility, and students must be equipped with the skills to think critically about this powerful technology.

Despite its remarkable advancements, GenAI is a tool and not a magical solution, so students need to recognize its limitations. Not everything is suited for AI-powered analysis, and blindly relying on it can have severe consequences. Critical thinking allows students to identify tasks for which GenAI is helpful and situations in which human judgment is indispensable. It is important that students approach GenAI outputs with a level of healthy skepticism, and it is the job of educators to teach students this highly relevant skill.

DEEPFAKES AND CRITICAL THINKING IN THE AGE OF AI

Though fake news has been an issue for some time, GenAI makes it easier to deceive people with deepfakes. Deepfakes are videos, images, and audio files that have been created using artificial intelligence to show someone doing or saying something that they did not actually do or say. Deepfakes can be used

to manipulate and threaten individuals, political figures, and companies. Because they seem to be authentic, deepfakes often create a visceral reaction within the viewer, inducing fear or anger. Deepfakes can be used to influence people in harmful ways.

Take this image that is included in a lesson on the dangers of deepfakes. The photo shows the Eiffel Tower in Paris, France, burning with the caption "Breaking News." During the lesson a teacher happened to walk into the classroom while it was displayed on the class's whiteboard. Upon seeing it, the teacher began weeping because

Created by Aaron Blackwelder via Canva.com

she had a summer trip planned to visit it in Paris and she believed the image to be true. Though this was an excellent display for students to see firsthand the impact deepfakes have on people, it also demonstrates the need for teachers to teach media literacy and critical thinking.

In the age of AI, images, videos, and audio clips are easily generated and shared on social media platforms. These platforms enable them to be spread quickly and reach millions of people before they are flagged and removed. Often, by the time the file is detected, the damage is done. Deepfakes are known to cause serious damage. Here are some of the problems they cause:

- **Misinformation and propaganda:** Deepfakes can be used to make it seem like someone said or did something they never did. They can be used to spread lies, sow discord, and manipulate public opinion.

- **Reputational damage:** Deepfakes can be used to create fake videos or audio of people that are embarrassing, offensive, or damaging to their reputation. They can have serious consequences for individuals' careers and personal lives.

- **Privacy violations:** Deepfake technology can be used to create realistic videos or audio recordings of people without their consent. This is a major privacy violation.

- **Erosion of trust:** Deepfakes can make it difficult to know what to believe online. This can erode trust in institutions and media and make it harder for people to have informed discussions about important issues.

Though there is no way to prevent deepfakes, we can learn how to identify them and help limit their spread while avoiding the pitfalls they create. Here are some ways you can teach students to be critical thinkers and identify deepfakes:

- **Healthy skepticism:** Start by emphasizing a critical approach to online information. Teach them to question what they see and hear online, especially if it seems too good (or bad) to be true. Provide students opportunities to view fake material and teach them to have a healthy skepticism.

- **Spot inconsistencies:** Deepfakes aren't perfect. Train students to look for the unnatural in an image or video, especially in faces and hands.
    - In videos, pay attention to blinking, smoothness of skin, and lip-syncing. Does the lighting and background seem consistent? Does the person's body language match their tone of voice?
    - In images, examine areas where detail is crucial. Is there the correct number of fingers? Do glasses sit on the face properly? Does jewelry, such as earrings, match?

- **Listen for the weird:** Deepfakes can alter audio as well. Voices may sound slightly off, robotic, or have strange inflections. Encourage students to pay attention to how natural the speech sounds.

- **Reverse image search and fact-checking:** Teach them about tools like reverse image search to see if the content appears elsewhere. Encourage them to consult trusted news sources to see if the video or claim has been debunked.

- **Consider the source:** Where did you find this video? Is it from a reputable source or a random account? Is the content believable given the context?

- **It's okay to not know:** Deepfakes are getting more sophisticated. If something feels off, but they can't pinpoint why, encourage them to discuss it with a trusted adult or wait before sharing.

Look at this image of the Pope in a puffer jacket. The image quickly became viral over social media in 2023. Many thought the pontiff had a new style and had forsaken his traditional garments. However, the image was AI-generated. This is a harmless example of a deepfake. This picture injured no one's reputation. But clearly, it is a fake and there are tells that the discerning eye can find. Look at the Pope's glasses. The lens on his right side is warped on the edge. The crucifix is hanging from just half a chain. The way he is holding his coffee cup defies the laws of physics.

By teaching students these strategies, we can equip them with the necessary skills to navigate the complexities of the modern media landscape, fostering a generation of responsible consumers of information.

Equipping students with critical thinking skills is not just about navigating the complexities of GenAI; it's about preparing them for a future where technology is

Pablo Xavier (2023) via Midjourney

ubiquitous. By becoming critical consumers of GenAI, students can leverage its benefits while maintaining an awareness that GenAI can produce inaccurate, biased, or unclear information. This awareness will help shape a future where GenAI serves humanity, not the other way around.

Issues around deepfakes and ethical use of GenAI will intensify in the coming years and not just in education. As GenAI improves it will become more challenging to identify improper use. This is why it is essential to teach students how to use GenAI ethically.

Students will use GenAI whether they are taught to or not. They need to understand how to use GenAI ethically to prepare for their futures and in order to recognize when it is not being used in ethical ways.

CHAPTER REVIEW

The Big Ideas

Chapter 4 discussed the ethical and effective use of GenAI in education:

- Age-appropriate use: Consider the developmental stages of students and tailor GenAI use accordingly.

- Transparency: Be upfront with students about how and when GenAI is being used.

- Code of ethics: Develop a collaborative code of ethics to guide responsible GenAI use.

- Concerns with GenAI: Teach students to be critical consumers of GenAI. Teach the ABCs:
  - Is it Accurate?
  - What Biases are present?
  - Is it Clearly communicating my intent?

- Fact-checking and verification: Challenge students to be critical when using GenAI outputs.

- Lateral reading: Lateral reading encourages students to explore beyond the initial source and verify the information.

It is important to have an ethical approach to integrating GenAI in the classroom. By fostering critical thinking skills and awareness of potential biases, teachers can help students become responsible users of GenAI and reap its benefits for learning.

You Try It: Create a Class Code of Conduct

Create a code of ethics with your students. Full directions are provided earlier in the chapter, but here is a reminder.

What You'll Need:

- Sticky notes and/or a whiteboard

- Student access to Google Forms or a similar tool for student voting

Instructions:

1. Review nonnegotiables: Mention school, district, and other policies regarding GenAI use that the students cannot change.

2. Brainstorm and categorize: Have students brainstorm lists of ways that generative AI might be used, and sort those lists into categories.

3. Discuss: In small groups or with the whole class, discuss which uses of generative AI are appropriate to use in class and which are not.

4. Vote: Have students use Google Forms or a similar tool to vote on which uses of generative AI are appropriate to use in class and which are not.

5. Compile, revise, and publish: Compile the results of student voting into an easy to read list of rules for generative AI in the classroom. If students have concerns or questions, make revisions until the class as a whole feels the document is complete. Publish this code of ethics somewhere students will be able to see it on a daily basis.

Questions for Reflection

1. Generative AI makes it difficult for teachers to determine what work is authentic to the student. How can we collaborate with students to ensure that their use of GenAI reflects their thinking?

2. Can you recall a time you used lateral reading to determine whether something was accurate? How might you help students use lateral reading to determine the accuracy of information?

3. We've now discussed the biases that can be reflected in GenAI systems. How can you mitigate potential bias in AI-generated content (e.g., lesson, text, questions, prompts) or recommendations for students?

4. Deepfakes are becoming very common. While some may be fun and entertaining, others can cause serious harm. What are some ways we can instill healthy skepticism in our students?

www.beyondthe curriculum.net/ book-1/chapter-4

Follow the link for more helpful resources related to the content found in Chapter 4.

ELEVATING LEARNING IN THE AGE OF AI

A Message From Aaron

Ms. Thompson was an eighth-grade ELA teacher in the building where I worked as an instructional coach. She was eager to support her students in completing a career research essay, but many of her students faced difficulties in writing. With short attention spans, many of them found the task of researching and completing the essay daunting. Given my familiarity with AI, Ms. Thompson sought my advice on how to leverage it to aid her students with the essay. After thinking through the parameters of the project and the students' needs, I proposed an idea that could provide the necessary support and scaffolding.

"Let's develop three chatbots for your students," I suggested. "We can program one to act as a research assistant, another to guide the writing process and help students draft their essays, and a third bot to provide feedback based on your rubric and assist with revisions."

Ms. Thompson was enthusiastic about the idea and wanted to understand more about its implementation.

I suggested we create a bot to act as a research assistant. We could program it to ask students their topic at the beginning of the chat. After students entered their topic, the bot would acknowledge their topic and follow up by asking, "What do you want to know about this topic?" and provide five different subtopics related to the topic. This would help students narrow their research. After students choose a subtopic, the bot would then ask, "Would you like to start with background information, statistics, quotes, or anecdotes about the topic?" Having students engage with the bot would enable them to get their research done quickly and efficiently and

(Continued)

(Continued)

help with executive functioning, as it wouldn't overwhelm them with an endless list of websites.

After they completed their research, students could engage with a bot that helps scaffold writing. I explained, "We can program the bot to assist in writing the essay, setting it up to support students through each paragraph. The initial question could be, 'What career are you interested in, and what are two to three reasons you selected this career?' The student could input their response, and the bot would generate three different opening paragraphs. Students then copy these paragraphs into a Google Doc, review each one, and highlight elements they like. After highlighting, they compose their introduction paragraph using the liked pieces from each version. We can extend this process to the body paragraphs and the conclusion."

Excited about the concept, Ms. Thompson expressed concerns about how parents might perceive AI's role in the writing process. She wanted to assure the parents that the project aimed to be rigorous and educational.

I reassured her, saying, "When students previously wrote this essay, they engaged in research and utilized graphic organizers with sentence frames—a combination of Level 1 and Level 2 Depth of Knowledge (DOK). By having the chatbot generate three versions and challenging students to select components they like, we're moving into Level 3 DOK (strategic thinking). Crafting their own version by integrating these components is Level 4 DOK (Extended thinking). I would assure any concerned parent that this approach is more rigorous and better prepares students for future careers, as they engage with AI and critically evaluate the output it generates."

Ms. Thompson loved the idea and enthusiastically agreed. We designed the chatbots and made them accessible to her students. As a result, all of her students were able to write their essays. Though some of them preferred to write them on their own, every student in the class was able to write an essay that represented their interests and learning.

AI, when used strategically, does not make tasks too easy for students. Instead, it can present more complex challenges, heightening rigor. What AI does streamline are mundane processes, freeing up time and mental bandwidth for students to focus on critical thinking skills.

Aaron

Artificial intelligence can't just be a quicker way to continue current education practices. Although GenAI does streamline many aspects of education for teachers and students, it should ultimately transform learning and assessment. As educators integrate AI into their classrooms, they need to consider the type of learning that is occurring and how to make their assignments resistant to easy completion by AI.

THE AI-PROOF ASSIGNMENT

Since the advent of ChatGPT teachers around the world have been concerned about students using AI to help them cheat on assignments. GenAI makes it easy for a student to complete some short answer questions, solve some basic math problems, or write major essays. And as technology advances, developers of AI detection tools cannot seem to keep up. So the question remains, how can teachers engage students in the age of AI without enticing them to use AI tools to cheat or blurring the lines between the parameters of the project and the capabilities of the tool, so that "cheating" is inevitable even if students don't have that intention?

The cheating problem is not new. According to the International Center for Academic Integrity (ICAI, 2024), in 2020 58 percent of students admitted to plagiarism, 64 percent admitted to cheating on tests, and 95 percent admitted to some form of cheating. These findings of the ICAI have been consistent since 1990.

The following are reasons most students cheat:

- the desire to get good grades

- the fear of failure

- procrastination or poor time management

- the belief they will not get caught

- lack of interest in the assignment

The cheating problem persists in the age of AI, too, and AI tools often make it easier for students to cheat on assignments.

In an op-ed titled "STUDENT VOICE: Teachers assign us to work that relies on rote memorization, then tell us not to use artificial intelligence," high school student Benjamin Weiss (2024) points out the issue is the work itself. Benjamin writes, "I regularly hear my classmates laugh about how they used ChatGPT for the prior night's homework. Their gloats are often accompanied by comments along the lines of 'Work smarter, not harder' and 'Teachers literally make it so easy to use AI.'" Teachers need to get away from assigning work that can easily be outsourced to AI, but first, we need to understand the capabilities and limitations of AI.

Look at the list below and consider which assignments AI is able to complete by itself:

1. Identify the main character, setting, plot, and conflict in a story.
2. Label the parts of a diagram or map.
3. Match the term and the definition for key vocabulary from the latest reading.
4. Solve a series of math problems using the Pythagorean theorem.
5. Classify different types of rocks based on their properties.
6. Compare and contrast two historical figures or events.
7. Calculate the area and volume of geometric shapes.
8. Summarize the main points of a scientific article.
9. Design and execute an experiment to test a hypothesis about plant growth.
10. Create a persuasive argument for or against a current issue.
11. Solve a multi-step word problem requiring analysis and application.
12. Write a critical response to a piece of art, music, or film.
13. Conduct independent research on a topic and present the findings.
14. Design a solution to a specific real-world problem in your community.
15. Use a mathematical model for data to predict an outcome and design solutions to improve the data.
16. Engage in a debate defending a stance on a controversial topic.

This list starts with relatively simple tasks that progressively become more and more complex. But which of these tasks can AI do? Below are the answers.

1. AI can identify basic elements of a story such as plot, character, conflict, and setting.
2. AI can label parts of a diagram or map.
3. AI can match vocabulary terms to definitions.
4. AI can solve a series of math problems.
5. AI can classify items.
6. AI can compare and contrast items.
7. AI can do basic calculations.
8. AI can summarize texts.

9. AI can help design an experiment, but a human will need to perform the experiment.

10. AI can create a persuasive argument, but it cannot use nuance to adapt it to a specific audience.

11. AI can solve multi-step problems, but humans are needed to consider complex situations.

12. AI can write a critical response, but deeper insights are limited.

13. AI cannot conduct independent research, such as interviews or surveys.

14. AI cannot design solutions to real-world problems within one's community.

15. AI can make predictions but cannot determine which solutions will benefit the user.

16. AI cannot engage in a live debate.

To understand which tasks AI can and cannot do we need to understand the Depth of Knowledge. Depth of Knowledge (DOK) is a framework used to categorize tasks based on the complexity of thinking required to complete them (Structural Learning, 2023). It is used to design assessments and curricula to promote deeper learning. Here's a breakdown of each level:

Level 1: Recall

Focuses on remembering and reproducing basic information.

Examples: Defining a term, listing facts, identifying elements in a story

Level 2: Skills and Concepts

Involves understanding and applying learned skills and concepts.

Examples: Explaining a process, summarizing information, and using formulas to solve problems

Level 3: Strategic Thinking

Demands planning, justification, and complex reasoning.

Examples: Analyzing data, drawing conclusions, supporting arguments with evidence, and solving problems in new situations

Level 4: Extended Thinking

Requires going beyond the learned material and applying it in new and creative ways.

Examples: Conducting research, designing solutions, evaluating the impact of an event, and making predictions based on evidence

Levels 1 and 2 DOK require limited thinking while Levels 3 and 4 require more critical analysis. The list of assignments above can be sorted into levels of DOK, as shown in Table 5.1.

TABLE 5.1 DEPTH OF KNOWLEDGE (DOK)

1 RECALL	2 SKILLS AND CONCEPTS	3 STRATEGIC THINKING	4 EXTENDED THINKING
1. Identify the main character, setting, plot, and conflict in a story. 2. Label the parts of a diagram or map. 3. Match the term and the definition for key vocabulary from the latest reading.	4. Solve a series of math problems using the Pythagorean theorem. 5. Classify different types of rocks based on their properties. 6. Compare and contrast two historical figures or events. 7. Calculate the area and volume of geometric shapes. 8. Summarize the main points of a scientific article.	9. Design and execute an experiment to test a hypothesis about plant growth. 10. Create a persuasive argument for or against a current issue. 11. Solve a multi-step word problem requiring analysis and application. 12. Write a critical response to a piece of art, music, or film. 13. Conduct independent research on a topic and present the findings.	14. Design a solution to a specific real-world problem in your community. 15. Use a mathematical model for data to predict an outcome and design solutions to improve the data. 16. Engage in a debate defending a stance on a controversial topic.

Teachers who want to AI-proof their assignments need to consider what kinds of assignments they are having students complete. Students need to have Level 1 and Level 2 knowledge to effectively engage in DOK 3 and 4, and teachers should continue to engage students in these kinds of activities. However, teachers should not limit their assignments to these.

According to Kun Yuan and Vi-Nhuan Le (2012), 90–97 percent of students are being assessed with Levels 1 and 2 in mathematics and English language arts while only 3–10 percent of U.S. elementary and secondary students are being assessed with Level 3 and Level 4 questions. This suggests that many teachers are creating tasks that are easily outsourced to AI. The best way to AI-proof an assignment is to consider the learning outcomes and redesign tasks to engage students at Levels 3 and 4 and then allow students to partner with AI to complete these tasks.

Table 5.2 includes suggestions to AI-proof an assignment:

ASSIGNMENTS PERFECT FOR AI	AI-PROOF ASSIGNMENTS
Identify basic elements of a story such as plot, character, conflict, and setting.	Rewrite a key scene from a different character's perspective, highlighting how this alteration impacts the overall plot progression and conflict resolution.
Label parts of a diagram or map.	Analyze and interpret a complex diagram or map. Then create a new one based on your understanding.
Match vocabulary terms to definitions.	Create a concept map that illustrates the relationships between the vocabulary terms, including how they interconnect and influence each other within a given context.
Solve a series of math problems.	Create real-world scenarios that require the application of the math concepts from the problems. Explain how each math problem relates to and can be used in these scenarios
Classify items.	Conduct research and choose a set of animals to categorize based on your assigned habitat.
Compare and contrast events.	Select two events and create a detailed timeline highlighting key aspects and consequences of each event. Additionally, include a reflection on the long-term implications of these events.
Complete basic calculations.	Analyze and interpret data sets to draw conclusions, supported by mathematical calculations.
Write summaries of texts.	Analyze and reimagine the text through the lens of a specific theme or concept.

Since GenAI can effectively complete the Level 1 and 2 DOK tasks that are essential to engaging in the Level 3 and 4 tasks, teachers should spend less time engaging students in those lower-level tasks. And when it is essential for students to learn these lower-level tasks, they should help build toward those higher-level tasks. When used well, GenAI can help create a more level playing field for students as it gives them equitable access to basic knowledge and information that can lead them to deeper learning opportunities. Thus, GenAI has the potential to provide equity for all students.

It has been noted that for various reasons, students of color are less likely to be engaged in rigorous DOK activities (Najarro, 2022). GenAI provides a bridge that will empower all students to engage in more rigorous tasks that will help them meet grade-level standards and become more college and career ready.

In the age of AI, what one knows becomes less important than what one can do with that knowledge. Students should be allowed to use AI to support their learning, and their work should be a blend of their thoughts intermixed with AI. Integrating AI into student work is a new approach to teaching and learning that will require updated assessment practices. But that leads to the question, how do we assess students in the age of AI?

THE PURPOSE OF ASSESSMENT

Typically letter grades such as A, B, C, D, and F or numbers such as 8/10 or 100% come to mind when people think of assessment. Others may think assessment is a score on the Smarter Balanced Assessment Consortium, iReady, or IXL tests. But are these truly an assessment of student learning?

The Latin root of the word assessment is *assidere*, which means "to sit beside." When we are assessing student learning we are sitting beside them, encouraging them, supporting their unique needs to help them grasp concepts. If we were teaching our children how to read and write we would not assign them points based on how well they demonstrate the learning. Rather, we would give them feedback such as, "I can see the effort you put into your work," or "I like the way you . . . next time, I want you to think about . . . " These phrases help reinforce and support learning.

Assessment is not about ranking students, grading students, or determining what college the student should go to. The point of assessment is to figure out what a student can and cannot do yet. It is to support growth and learning.

Grades and numbers detract from learning. In 1987, Ruth Butler ran an experiment to see the impact of grades on learning. She had four groups in her test:

- a group receiving comments only

- a group receiving grades only

- a group receiving praise only

- a group that received no feedback at all

In the pre-assessment, all groups performed similarly (see Table 5.3). However, during the post-assessment, the only students who demonstrated significant growth were those who received comments only. The students who received grades and praise showed similar negative impacts on learning as the students who received no feedback at all.

FEEDBACK CONDITION							
	Comments Only		Grades Only		Praise Only		No Feedback	
	High	Low	High	Low	High	Low	High	Low
SESSION 1								
Mean	19.55	10.16	19.28	10.28	19.68	9.92	19.48	10.00
Standard Deviation	4.20	3.35	5.05	6.48	6.47	5.04	5.36	3.36
SESSION 3								
Mean	25.04	14.92	14.92	7.32	13.60	9.96	11.76	8.36
Standard Deviation	5.22	5.23	6.06	2.84	4.38	3.76	5.42	2.69

Adapted from Butler (1987).

But the question remains, what if students were to receive feedback and grades? Won't this help support learning? Butler tested this idea and found that students who received both comments and grades underperformed students who received grades only, while students who received comments only once again demonstrated significant growth (see Table 5.4).

TABLE 5.4 BUTLER'S RESEARCH 1988

FEEDBACK CONDITION					
	Comments Only		Grades Only		Comments and Grades	
	High	Low	High	Low	High	Low
SESSION 1						
Mean	18.77	10.14	19.64	9.86	19.60	9.64
Standard Deviation	6.63	5.02	8.67	4.88	5.80	5.64
SESSION 3						
Mean	24.27	13.50	16.45	8.59	11.82	5.82
Standard Deviation	6.70	7.79	9.34	6.41	5.26	5.40

Adapted from Butler (1988).

What is it about providing comments that helps drive learning that grades seem to miss? Grading lacks the human touch. Most teachers spend time away from students reviewing student work and marking what is correct and incorrect to come up with a score or a grade. There is no conversation involved in this process. However, comments without grades point out what was done well, what was done incorrectly, and what could be done to improve the overall work. They are personal notes that communicate how the teacher cares for the student and their learning.

GenAI can help generate some of these comments and streamline other responsibilities teachers have so they can spend more time conferencing with students about their work.

A FOCUS ON FEEDBACK

Providing rich feedback is essential to fostering the student-teacher relationship. When done well, focused, actionable feedback informs students what they are doing well and what they can improve upon.

Feedback should focus on specific behaviors or actions of the student and not come across as a personal attack. The feedback needs to be clear and specific while providing suggestions for improvement. An excellent framework for providing feedback is Mark Barnes's SE2R formula (Barnes, 2015, p. 58). This is a simple approach with four steps:

1. **Summarize.** Provide a one- or two-sentence statement of what was accomplished.

   Example: "I noticed you provided several pieces of research in your project that will help build a strong argument."

2. **Explain.** Give a detailed objective explanation of what learning is demonstrated and/or what is missing, based on the activity guidelines.

   Example: "However, you did not include any citations in your work. Citing sources is important because it gives credit where credit is due, and it can help your reader to learn more by visiting your sources."

3. **Redirect.** Point students to specific areas they need to work on and either reattempt or revise the work. Check for understanding. When there is a misunderstanding this can become an opportunity to reteach.

   Example: "I want you to go back and add your sources. Do you know how to do this?"

4. Resubmit. Ask the student to resubmit after making changes. This allows the teacher to reassess.

Example: "Once you do this, please resubmit your work. I look forward to your revisions."

Teachers can provide other forms of feedback by including comments on student work in the margins. In most digital learning management systems (LMS) such as Canvas, Blackboard, or Google Classroom, a comments section is typically provided. Teachers can use these comment sections to highlight strengths and provide suggestions for student growth.

Feedback needs to be actionable—something students can use to improve their work and further their learning. Using a structure like SE2R centers feedback on objective goals and helps provide clear solutions. This helps students see how they can grow as learners.

AN EMPHASIS ON DECISION MAKING AND REFLECTION

In this new era, AI can easily generate products for us. It can produce documents, images, videos, and more. It can even produce an entire slide deck detailing the lifecycle of a butterfly with a few clicks—and it does a pretty good job. However, the human touch is needed for AI to complete the task in a way that caters to one's audience and purpose. Because of this, students need to learn how to evaluate AI-generated outputs and learn how to be decision makers. Though AI can do a good job creating products for them, it is the process and decisions they make that help ensure that what is generated reflects the intended purpose.

In the opening of this chapter, a story was shared about Ms. Thompson. Her students used AI to help craft a career research essay. When they finish the final draft, the essay should easily meet the guidelines so assessing the writing seems redundant. Instead, we need to consider new standards to assess student learning as they use AI to assist them with these processes.

Ms. Thompson's students prompted a chatbot to write multiple versions of each paragraph. After the bot produced the paragraphs, students copied them into a Google Doc and highlighted what they liked about each version using the Comments tool. Students explained what they liked about their selections and then synthesized their paragraphs from the AI models.

Having AI produce these exemplars helps teach students how to write. Having them highlight what they liked and explain why they liked it required higher-order thinking—Level 3 DOK. Students are making decisions about their selection based on what best fits their audience and purpose while communicating these ideas in ways that express their personalities. After highlighting, they synthesized their piece of writing based on the ideas AI generated—Level 4 DOK. Though AI assisted students with the composition of the essay, students were doing high-level work by thinking intentionally about what would go into the final draft of their essays. Therefore, teachers need to shift from assessing an outcome to challenging and assessing students during the process.

Along with the final draft of the essay, Ms. Thompson had her students submit the planning document with annotations and a link to the chat with the chatbot to assess how her students partnered with AI. She wanted to know to what degree her students relied on the chatbot to do the work for them. Ms. Thompson wanted to know if students were using it to do the work for them or if they were using it to inspire and further their thinking.

This led to the development of a rubric that assessed the students' process. Ultimately, two rubrics were developed: one to assess the degree of student independence with AI (Table 5.5) and the second to assess the student depth of learning with AI (Table 5.6). These helped her set learning goals with her students to support and challenge them. She wanted to ensure students used AI as a thought partner, allowing them to express their ideas effectively and critically.

Using GenAI should not simply make schoolwork easier for students. Rather, it should help streamline some of the mundane tasks to enable students to engage in more critical thinking and higher-order tasks. Students should reflect on how, when, and why they are using GenAI. They will learn more as a result, especially when asked to justify specific decisions they make.

Teachers should focus on providing rich and meaningful feedback. Assessing higher-level thinking skills can be approached as having a dialogue with students about their thinking. GenAI may be able to create some products and complete lower-level tasks, but it cannot replicate genuine student thinking. Educators who embrace the idea of assessment as "sitting beside their students" will take student learning and critical thinking to new heights.

STUDENT DECISION MAKING WITH AI-GENERATED PRODUCTS			
LEVEL 1: EMERGING	LEVEL 2: APPROACHING	LEVEL 3: MEETING	LEVEL 4: EXCELLING
Students can do this with full assistance.	Students can do this with some assistance.	Students can do this independently.	Students can collaborate with others in doing this.
CRITERIA	OBJECTIVES		STUDENT SCORE
Intentional Decision-Making Process	The student . . . makes strategic changes that significantly impact the output based on specific goals and criteria. uses a variety of editing and revising techniques (e.g., word choice, sentence structure, organization) strategically and intentionally.		
Justifying Decisions	The student . . . explains how each change enhances the product. provides the reasoning behind each change, drawing specific connections to the purpose and audience. identifies areas for improvement and explains how chosen strategies address those areas. demonstrates a strong understanding of how changes impact overall effectiveness.		
Ability to Synthesize	The student . . . makes edits and revisions that result in a highly polished and unified text. Includes transitions that effectively link ideas and maintain a clear focus throughout. demonstrates a strong awareness of the audience and purpose.		

STUDENT DECISION MAKING WITH AI-GENERATED PRODUCTS			
	LEVEL 1: RECALL & REPRODUCTION	**LEVEL 2: BASIC APPLICATION**	**LEVEL 3: STRATEGIC THINKING**	**LEVEL 4: EXTENDED THINKING**
Intentional Decision-Making Process	Student can prompt AI to generate an output.	Prompt engineering is intentional and focused on the intended task and purpose.	Prompt engineering demonstrates an awareness of AI's limitations and applies multiple prompts to achieve desired outcomes.	Student analyzes biases in the outputs and seeks to integrate other sources to be considerate of diverse perspectives.
Integration of AI Outputs	Student writes a simple restatement of AI output that may use synonyms or varying sentence structures.	Student applies editing techniques to AI outputs (e.g., word choice, sentence structure, organization) to include in their work.	Student makes revisions to or combines AI outputs and includes them in intentional ways in their work to meet specific goals and criteria.	Student makes strategic changes to AI outputs and combines them with other data to create novel works that respond to diverse perspectives and audiences.
Justifying Decisions	Student provides simple explanations to justify decision making.	Student explains how each change enhances the work.	Student provides reasoning behind each change, drawing specific connections to the purpose and audience.	The student defends their decisions, drawing on diverse data sources and expert opinions in their reasoning.

This rubric is based on Webb's Depth of Knowledge and reflects DOK levels 1–4. Adapted from Webb (1997).

The Big Ideas

Chapter 5 discussed the future of AI and how to elevate learning by asking students to complete tasks requiring higher-level thinking skills.

- Streamline education: AI will streamline many aspects of education for teachers and students.

- Higher-level thinking skills: AI will challenge educators to prioritize higher-level thinking skills and critical thinking. Educators should design assignments that require these skills.

- Feedback is better: Comments and feedback are more likely to improve student learning than letter grades or numbers.

- Assess the process: Assess students' decision making, thinking, and reflection during the process of using GenAI tools.

- Timely feedback: Feedback needs to be timely and actionable to be useful.

- Understand GenAI's limits: It is important to understand the capabilities and limitations of GenAI.

- Focus on relationships: Promote a positive classroom culture and strong student-teacher relationships.

- Emphasize human thinking: GenAI can create products, but human thinking is crucial to ensure the products match their goal and audience.

You Try It: AI-Proof an Assignment

Take an existing assignment and tweak it to focus on higher-level thinking skills.

What You'll Need:

- Access to GenAI such as ChatGPT or Gemini

- A unit or lesson you would like to make more resistant to AI

Instructions:

1. Choose your assignment. Choose an assignment you are worried about becoming obsolete or easily completed with GenAI. If you can't think of a particular assignment, you can always ask GenAI to come up with some example assignments to practice on. (Review examples from Chapter 2 if you need a reminder.)

2. Analyze the assignment to determine the current Depth of Knowledge (DOK). Figure out where the assignment currently sits on the DOK chart earlier in this chapter. Remember that GenAI can easily complete DOK level 1 and 2 tasks. If you are more comfortable with a different framework for higher-level thinking skills, such as Bloom's Taxonomy, use that instead.

(Continued)

(Continued)

3. Revise the task to increase the DOK. Look at the charts earlier in this chapter to come up with ideas.

   Alternatively, you can ask your preferred GenAI platform for some help with the following prompt: "Here is an assignment I have used in the past. I would like to teach the same concepts in a different way. Can you look at this assignment and suggest other ways to teach the same content?" Understand that not all of the new examples will be a higher DOK.

4. Review the new task to ensure continuity. Make sure that the new assignment meets your original learning objectives. If it does not, return to step 3 and continue revisions.

5. Consider how you will assess the new assignment. How will you know that students have met your learning objectives for this assignment? Consider the following questions as you think about assessment:

   - How will students receive feedback on this assignment? Will it be a number in a gradebook? Written comments? An individual conference with the student?

   - Consider when students will receive feedback. Will feedback be given only after the assignment is due, or will students receive feedback while they are doing the work?

   - Can GenAI help provide students with feedback or guidance on their work?

   - Will students use GenAI tools as part of this assignment? If so, consider having students reflect on their use of GenAI tools, maybe using something like the "Student Decision Making with AI-Generated Products" rubric in Table 5.6.

Revising assignments in this way will help challenge students and elevate the learning in your classroom.

Questions for Reflection

1. Think of one assignment you currently use that could be "AI-proofed." How would you modify it according to the recommendations from the chapter?

2. The chapter proposes a shift from traditional grading to a focus on rich feedback. How can you incorporate more effective feedback mechanisms into your teaching practices?

3. The example of Ms. Thompson's students using a chatbot to write an essay highlights the idea of partnering with AI. How can you encourage your students to use AI as a tool to enhance their learning, rather than a crutch?

4. The chapter talks about how AI will change the role of teachers. How do you see the role of a teacher evolving with the increased use of AI in the classroom?

Follow the link or scan the QR code for more helpful resources related to the content found in Chapter 5.

CONCLUSION
Now What?

Generative AI is a powerful tool that is increasingly becoming part of everyday life. Both students and teachers can use GenAI to increase their efficiency and communicate their thinking more effectively. Through this book, the authors have showcased effective ways to use AI. Using GenAI should become a cornerstone of instructional practice rather than an exciting idea to try once and then shelve. Here are some recommendations to integrate AI into normal practice.

1. **Use GenAI regularly.** Whether it is to clarify an email, plan a lesson, or help students with feedback using a customized chatbot, frequent use will improve the quality and usefulness of the AI outputs.

2. **Be upfront with stakeholders about AI use, including students.** Generative AI needs to be viewed as a normal tool, like spellcheck and graphing calculators, rather than something that is taboo or hidden.

3. **Show students how GenAI performs on projects and assignments.** This dialogue will enable students to see the limitations of AI firsthand and will be a great reminder to teachers to continue emphasizing higher-order thinking skills.

4. **Finally, emphasize that the purpose of school is learning.** GenAI can help students express and communicate their thinking, but it can't think for them.

Time is our most valuable and scarce resource. Because of GenAI, teachers can have more time to interact in positive ways with their students, as it will alleviate some of the low-level work for both students and teachers. Adding AI to the classroom helps increase the ability of teachers to work directly with students, thus enhancing the human-centered activities that will help classrooms thrive.

The most important thing a teacher can do is build a culture of inclusion and promote a sense of belonging while maintaining high expectations.

Zaretta Hammond used the term *warm demander* to describe teachers who possess personal warmth paired with high expectations. By maximizing the potential of GenAI tools, teachers can get back some time in their schedules, which can be used to establish this culture and build strong relationships with students, enabling teachers to become warm demanders. Centering on positive relationships between teachers and students helps foster safe learning environments and builds equitable opportunities for students.

Equity ensures that education is accessible, meaningful, and relevant. Because of GenAI, every student can have an on-demand tutor regardless of where they live and what their schedule might be. Students can learn at their own pace and in different languages. GenAI can support diverse learning styles and offer a variety of formats, such as text-to-speech or other accessibility tools, for students who need them. Students can personalize support to access materials at different levels and get extra help when assignments seem out of reach. All of this helps provide further access to learning to meet the needs of every student.

Most jobs today do not require candidates to be able to navigate the landscape of GenAI. However, this is rapidly changing. Because it helps streamline many of our rudimentary tasks and increases productivity, it is clear that employers will eventually expect employees to be fluent in AI. One of the most important roles educators play in a child's life is to help prepare students to engage in the world and be relevant. Teaching students to use GenAI effectively and ethically will help students as they prepare for their futures.

Not only does AI help prepare students for their futures, but it allows teachers to create more meaningful learning opportunities today. Teachers can also leverage GenAI to help meet students' diverse needs. It can help teachers keep their content fresh. GenAI can provide teachers access to strategies and resources that can help them make deeper impacts in the lives of their students. Teachers have access to a thought partner they can collaborate with to create lesson plans and student activities and improve their craft through reflective conversation.

Ultimately, equity means that education improves for everyone, not just in areas with more resources and better-trained staff. In the Age of AI, teachers can be more flexible with *how* students demonstrate learning while setting high expectations for learning. Adding AI to the classroom will not lower the bar, but instead it will raise the bar and promote personalized rigor for everyone.

REFERENCES

Arce, S. (2019). Exploring parent and teacher perceptions of family engagement. *International Journal of Teacher Leadership, 10*(2), 82–94. https://files.eric.ed.gov/fulltext/EJ1244923.pdf

Barnes, M. (2015). *Assessment 3.0: Throw out your grade book and inspire learning.* SAGE.

Bohannon, M. (2023, June 8). *Lawyer used ChatGPT in court—and cited fake cases. A judge is considering sanctions.* Forbes. Retrieved June 27, 2024, from https://www.forbes.com/sites/mollybohannon/2023/06/08/lawyer-used-chatgpt-in-court-and-cited-fake-cases-a-judge-is-considering-sanctions

Butler, R. (1987). Task-involving and ego-involving properties of evaluation: Effects of different feedback conditions on motivational perceptions, interest, and performance. *Journal of Educational Psychology, 79*(4), 474–482. https://doi.org/10.1037/0022-0663.79.4.474

Butler, R. (1988). Enhancing and undermining intrinsic motivation: The effects of task-involving and ego-involving evaluation of interest and performance. *British Journal of Educational Psychology, 58*(1), 1–14. https://doi.org/10.1111/j.2044-8279.1988.tb00874.x

Constantino, S. (2016, February 1). *Visible family engagement.* The Constantino Group. Retrieved June 27, 2024, from https://drsteveconstantino.com/visible-family-engagement/

Google. (2023). *Gemini* [Large language model]. gemini.google.com/share/d18f35510fe5

Hammond, Z. L. (2015). *Culturally responsive teaching and the brain.* Corwin.

Hawe, E., & Dixon, H. (2023, November 8). *How to use exemplars and rubrics to improve student outcomes.* Research Outreach. Retrieved June 27, 2024, from https://researchoutreach.org/articles/exemplars-rubrics-improve-student-outcomes/

Hughes, A. (2023, September 25). *ChatGPT: Everything you need to know about OpenAI's GPT-4 tool.* BBC Science Focus. Retrieved June 27, 2024, from https://www.sciencefocus.com/future-technology/gpt-3/

International Center for Academic Integrity. (2024). *Facts and statistics.* International Center for Academic Integrity. Retrieved June 27, 2024, from https://academicintegrity.org/resources/facts-and-statistics

Jesutofunmi, O. A., Lester, J. C., Spichak, S., Rotemberg, V., & Daneshjou, R. (2023, October 20). *Large language models propagate race-based medicine.* NPJ Digital Medicine. Retrieved June 27, 2024, from https://www.nature.com/articles/s41746-023-00939-z

Lin, L. (2024, May 15). *A quarter of U.S. teachers say AI tools do more harm than good in K–12 education.* Pew Research Center. Retrieved June 27, 2024, from https://www.pewresearch.org/short-reads/2024/05/15/a-quarter-of-u-s-teachers-say-ai-tools-do-more-harm-than-good-in-k-12-education/

Lucas, G. (Director). (1980). *Star wars: The empire strikes back* [Film]. Lucas Films.

Mollick, E. (2023, September 24). *Everyone is above average.* One Useful Thing. Retrieved June 27, 2024, from https://www.oneusefulthing.org/p/everyone-is-above-average

Najarro, I. (2022, January 13). Teachers deliver less to students of color, study finds. Is bias the reason? *Education Week*. Retrieved June 27, 2024, from https://www.edweek.org/teaching-learning/teachers-deliver-less-to-students-of-color-study-finds-is-bias-the-reason/2022/01

Noy, S., & Zhang, W. (2023, March 10). *Experimental evidence on the productivity effects of generative artificial intelligence.* MIT Economics. Retrieved June 27, 2024, from https://economics.mit.edu/sites/default/files/inline-files/Noy_Zhang_1_0.pdf

O'Malley, J. (2023, April 9). *ChatGPT is the real deal—and it's going to change the world.* TechFinitive. Retrieved June 27, 2024, from https://www.techfinitive.com/features/chatgpt-is-going-to-change-the-world/

OpenAI. (n.d.). *How ChatGPT and our language models are developed.* OpenAI Help Center. Retrieved June 27, 2024, from https://help.openai.com/en/articles/7842364-how-chatgpt-and-our-language-models-are-developed

OpenAI. (2023, November). *Terms of use: Effective January, 31, 2024.* https://openai.com/policies/row-terms-of-use/

Prothero, A. (2024, March 12). *What is age-appropriate use of AI? 4 developmental stages to know about.* Education Week. https://www.edweek.org/technology/what-is-age-appropriate-use-of-ai-4-developmental-stages-to-know-about/2024/02

Rogers, R. (2023, April 20). *What's AGI, and why are AI experts skeptical?* WIRED. Retrieved June 27, 2024, from https://www.wired.com/story/what-is-artificial-general-intelligence-agi-explained/

Structural Learning. (2023, May 11). *Webb's depth of knowledge.* Retrieved June 27, 2024, from https://www.structural-learning.com/post/webbs-depth-of-knowledge

University of Massachusetts Global. (n.d.). *The true impact of teacher turnover.* Retrieved June 27, 2024, from https://www.umassglobal.edu/news-and-events/blog/teacher-turnover

Walker, S. M. (2023, September 1). *Everything we know about GPT-4.* Klu.ai. Retrieved June 27, 2024, from https://klu.ai/blog/gpt-4-llm

Walton, E. (2023, November 9). *Performance declines in basic mathematics and reading skills since the COVID-19 pandemic are evident across many racial/ethnic groups.* National Center for Education Statistics. Retrieved June 27, 2024, from https://nces.ed.gov/nationsreportcard/blog/pandemic_performance_declines_across_racial_and_ethnic_groups.aspx

Webb, Norman. (1997). *Criteria for alignment of expectations and assessments in mathematics and science education.* Research Monograph No. 6. National Institute for Science Education.

Weiss, B. (2024, April 29). *Student voice: Teachers assign us work that relies on rote memorization, then tell us not to use artificial intelligence.* The Hechinger Report. https://hechingerreport.org/student-voice-teachers-assign-us-work-that-relies-on-rote-memorization-then-tell-us-not-to-use-artificial-intelligence/

Yuan, K., & Le, V.-N. (2012, February). *Estimating the percentage of students who were exposed to deeper learning on the state achievement tests.* Rand Education. Retrieved June 27, 2024, from https://www.hewlett.org/wp-content/uploads/2016/08/Estimating_Percentage_Students_Tested_on_Cognitively_Demanding_Items_Through_the_State_Achievement_Tests_RAND_3_2012.pdf

INDEX

CORWIN
A Sage Company

Confident Teachers, *Inspired* Learners

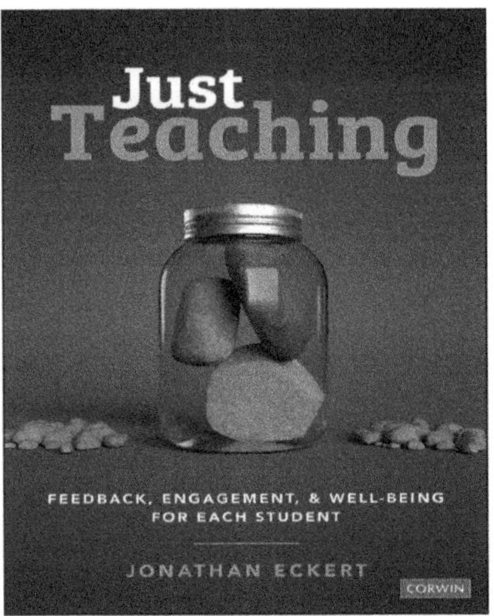

JONATHAN ECKERT

Focus on feedback, engagement, and well-being to support comprehensive growth while elevating the essential work of educators.

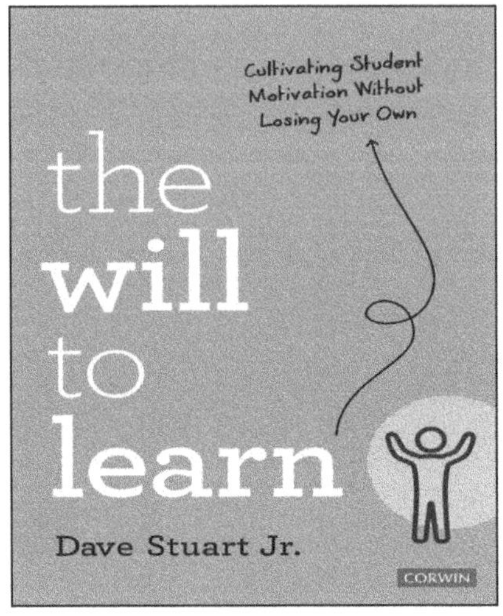

DAVE STUART JR.

Discover how teachers and schools can cultivate the conditions in which students want to do the work of learning with care.

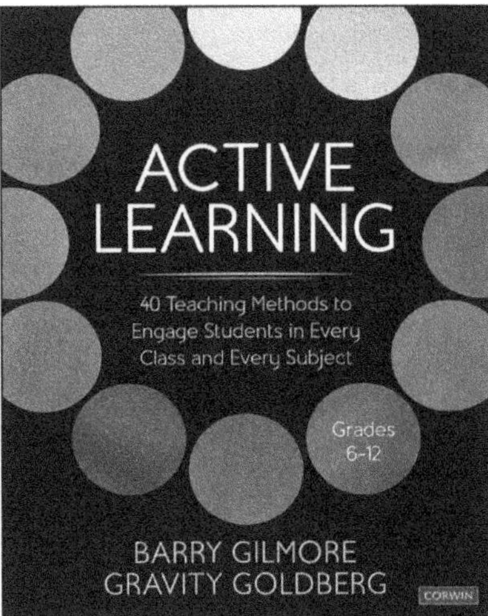

BARRY GILMORE, GRAVITY GOLDBERG

Boost student engagement with this go-to guide for designing active and engaging learning experiences.

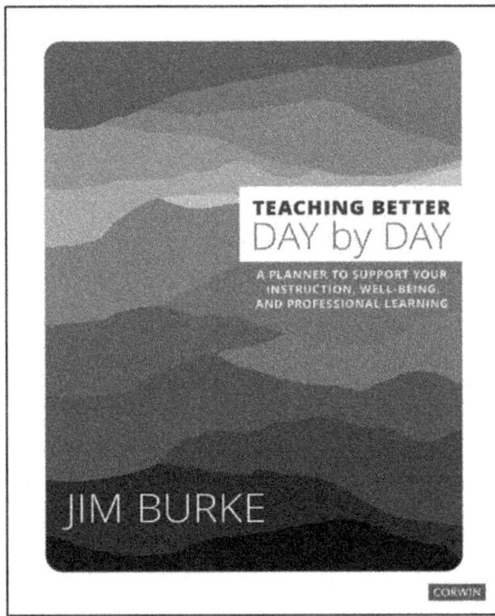

JIM BURKE

Manage your time, your classes, and your life with these yearly, monthly, weekly, and daily planning pages to achieve personal and professional goals.

To order your copies, visit **corwin.com/teachingessentials**

No matter where you are in your professional journey, Corwin books provide accessible strategies that benefit ALL learners—and ease the many demands teachers face.

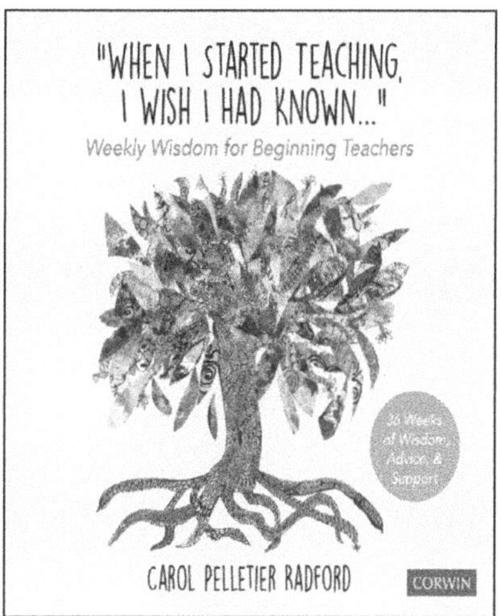

CAROL PELLETIER RADFORD

Support beginning teachers with this collection of advice throughout the 36 weeks of their first teaching year—and beyond!

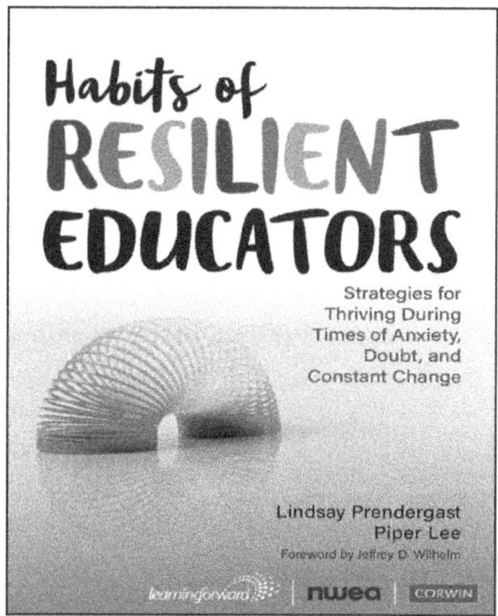

LINDSAY PRENDERGAST, PIPER LEE

Help educators sustain teaching habits to set up students for success and to be the best version of themselves in the classroom.

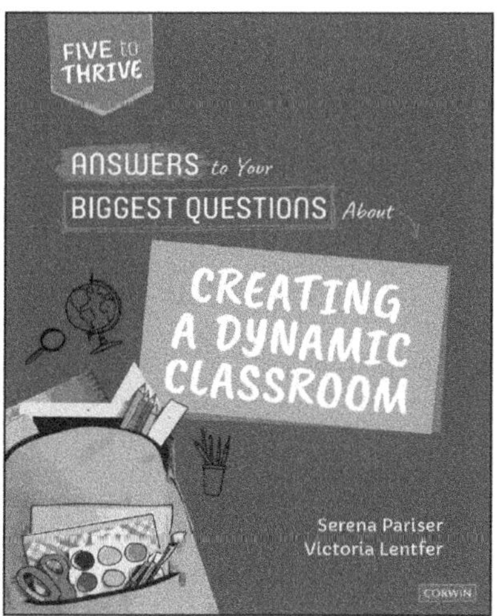

SERENA PARISER, VICTORIA LENTFER

Find actionable solutions to classroom management and culture, engaging lesson design, and effective communication.

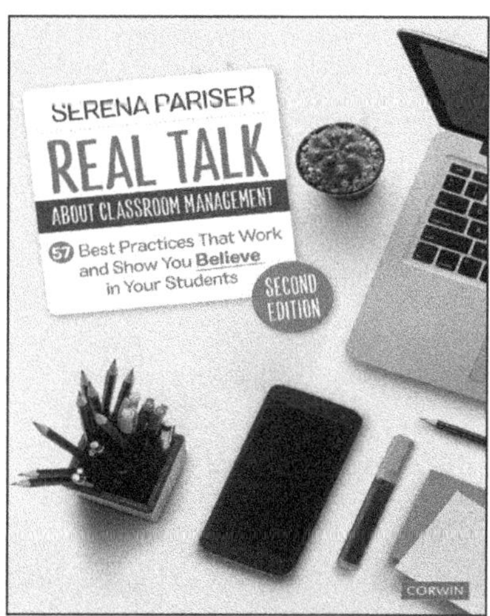

SERENA PARISER

Build positive relationships in the classroom with planned instruction that engages interest and nurtures independence to be successful in school.

CORWIN